Literacy for Living

BOOK TWO

Anne Vize

PHOENIX
EDUCATION

First published in Australia in 2003

PHOENIX EDUCATION PTY LTD
Melbourne
PO Box 197, Albert Park 3206
Tel: (03) 9699 8377 Fax: (03) 9699 9242
Sydney
PO Box 3141, Putney 2112
Tel: (02) 9809 3579 Fax: (02) 9808 1430

www.phoenixeduc.com

ISBN 1 876580 61 5

Printed in Australia by Five Senses Education

Contents

About Literacy for Living

Literacy for Living: Book 2 is an English resource book for teachers of older adolescents and young adults with special learning needs. The aim of the book is to extend key literacy skills through a range of activities focused on practical life skills. It contains four short stories and a range of accompanying worksheets and suggested activities with themes that are central to the lives of older teens and young adults growing up in Australia today. It is a valuable resource for mainstream and specialist teachers working with young people who need extra assistance with their literacy and English program. The central themes covered in the book include topics as diverse as:

- attraction and falling in love
- body image
- being independent
- moving out of home
- finding work
- sharing a house
- dealing with parents
- managing relationships
- success and failure

The book also provides activity suggestions and worksheets on a large number of practical living topics. These are designed to help students to develop their skills for independent living, and increase their ability to manage day-to-day tasks. They also help students to learn some of the key words and phrases associated with daily living tasks. Some of the practical living skills topics covered in the book include:

- job seeking skills
- writing skills for work
- setting up a house
- sharing household tasks
- dealing with housemates
- budgeting
- cooking skills
- cleaning tasks
- map reading
- shopping

Literacy for Living: Book 2 is designed to be used in one of two ways:

- as a stand-alone resource book where individual students can work through the stories and relevant activities at their own pace with the support of a teacher
- as an accompaniment to general classroom materials where the whole class can participate in activities and worksheets which support particular classroom themes

Who is it for?

This book has been designed to extend students who have undertaken activities from Book 1, and are ready to move on to new tasks. It has also been designed for students who are from an older age group but whose literacy skills are not at a level typically expected from students of their chronological age. These students will enjoy the stories and activities in Book Two because they are about topics which are suited to their age group and level of understanding, but do not require a high level of literacy.

There are many groups of students who will benefit from the activities in this book. These include students:

- who need extra help with their literacy skills
- who are learning English as a second language
- with an intellectual disability
- with a learning disability or other special learning need
- who have missed extended or critical periods of schooling
- who require additional support with their English program
- who are learning about living skills

These students might be attending a mainstream secondary school, special school, post-school education setting, supported living or educational program, or be undertaking further study for their own interests. They may be able to progress through the entire book, or might prefer to participate only in activities that are suited to their skills and interests.

What is in the book?

The book is divided into four separate units of work, each comprising a short story, worksheets and suggested activities, and a learning checklist.

Unit 1: Pak and Jimmy's Place

This story is about two young adults who have moved out of home for the first time. They are living in shared accommodation, and receive support to participate in community activities and daily living tasks. The story follows them through a typical week. Pak works at a factory as a cleaner, and enjoys spending time with his girlfriend, Sarah. Jimmy works in a supported employment program and enjoys fishing, playing cricket and catching the train to visit his mum.

This unit can be used to teach topics such as being independent, sharing a house, organising belongings, managing time, planning activities and using public transport. It is useful for prompting students to start thinking about moving out of home and on to the next stage in their lives. It can also be used to introduce some basic work concepts, and as a starting point for further learning on job seeking skills, such as those discussed in 'Out of Work'.

Unit 2: First Impressions

This story is about a young woman who falls in love with a young man at her TAFE. Frances is a fairly non-descript teenager who has never taken much pride in her appearance. The young man, Brett, is the most popular person at TAFE, and is generally the centre of attention. Frances has several unsuccessful attempts at impressing Brett, until she finally realises the futility of her endeavours. Frances eventually finds herself in a position to help Brett out, and he suddenly sees her in a new light. The ending of the story is left unstated, which provides an opportunity for students to draw their own conclusions.

This unit can be used to explore issues such as physical attraction, creating a good impression, the importance of looks and personality, self-esteem and individuality. On a practical level, students can learn about the words and language associated with topics such as clothing, appearance, activities, post school education, friendships and relationships.

Unit 3: Out of Work

In this story, we meet Toula, who is well on the way to giving her career counsellor a nervous breakdown. Toula is every employer's nightmare. She is loud, rude, poorly dressed and often late. Ellen, Toula's career counsellor, is determined that she is going to find Toula a job. The story follows Toula through a number of job applications, until she is finally accepted for a traineeship at the local botanical gardens.

This unit is ideal for students who are learning about the world of work. It covers topics such as preparing for an interview, applying for a job, writing skills at work, job seeking strategies, planning and organising a work day and fields of employment.

Unit 4: Moving Out

This story is about a young couple who move out of home to share a house. Gina is from a Greek background and her mother is not happy about her moving in with her boyfriend before they are married. Gina is determined that things are going to work out in their new house, and impatient to be free of the restrictions of life with her mother. Her boyfriend, Jake, struggles just to pack his belongings and get them to the house on moving day. However, once they are all at the house together, it is Jake who manages to restore calm and to make Gina's mother feel that her daughter is not really leaving her.

This unit can be used to talk about topics such as moving out of home for the first time, relationships, expectations of parents and family members, cultural differences and sharing tasks and responsibilities. On a practical level, students can participate in activities and complete worksheets on topics such as household safety, Australian slang, recipes and cooking tasks, designing a house, real estate language and using appliances safely in the house.

Reading the stories

The short stories can be photocopied and supplied to students individually, or they can be read by the teacher to a class group. It is important that teachers are aware of the particular needs and reading skills of their students before making the decision to ask students to read aloud, particularly to a group of their peers. Many students who are quite competent readers find such a request intimidating, and for students with poor reading skills it can be a terrifying prospect. It can be useful to ask students if they are comfortable reading aloud before beginning work on a story. If a student indicates that he or she is not happy to read aloud, respect their decision. Avoid forcing a student to read aloud, as this will generally only create resentment and anxiety. Teachers and students alike are generally aware of the gaps in skills which exist for particular students without this fact being highlighted to a whole class group. For some students, the positive effect that occurs as a result of being able to simply enjoy

Literacy for Living: Book 2 (Phoenix Education) © Anne Vize 2003 listening to a story without any pressure to read aloud can provide a significant boost to their enthusiasm for and interest in reading. If teachers do nothing more than create an interest in reading where none existed previously, they have done well.

Learning checklists

As for Book One, each unit of work ends with a learning checklist. This list can be used as a record of tasks undertaken by students as part of each unit. The checklist can be managed by the teacher or the student, and can be retained as an assessment record. Students may like to negotiate with teachers on which tasks they are going to complete, and in what time frame. This places responsibility for learning with students, and helps them to see themselves as owners of their own work and achievements.

Worksheets and activities

Before reading the story

In each unit of work, there are a number of pre-reading activity suggestions. These activities introduce important concepts in the story, and provide a useful check for teachers that the unit will be at an appropriate level for their students.

Activities for beginning readers

These tasks require little or no reading and writing skills from students. The activities primarily involve discussion or the use of pictures or diagrams to convey meaning, rather than the use of text. Some of the activities may be useful for teaching key words and labels for common household or work-based objects. The activities are designed to provide sufficient content for a student who is not able to read to still be able to participate in a unit of work along with the rest of a group.

Word skills

The worksheets in this section cover a range of skill areas and ability levels. Some of the tasks require a similar level of literacy to those contained in Book One, while others are slightly more demanding. The focus of this section is on teaching and reinforcing basic word skills such as alphabetical order, word groupings, recognising common letter blends and using a dictionary or personal knowledge to find definitions. Students are encouraged to use existing strategies for reading new words, and to use their own knowledge of words to explain meanings.

Comprehension

The questions and activities in the Comprehension section aim to extend students beyond giving simple factual responses. In addition to the 'True and False' questions of Book One, there are a number of worksheets that ask students to think about their perceptions of particular situations or scenes from the stories.

Writing skills

The topics covered in this section provide students with opportunities to practise a number of different styles and forms of writing. Topics covered include writing at work, resumes, describing personal qualities, writing character profiles and writing lists of tasks. There are also creative writing tasks which allow students to explore other genres such as poetry.

Speaking and listening

This section provides structured learning tasks which focus on organising thoughts and constructing meaningful conversation and speech. Students can participate in activities such as solving problems and making decisions, discussing issues, expressing opinions and planning household and work-related tasks. Many of the activities ask students to work in small groups or with a partner. This format is ideal for extending students' abilities to manage the speaking and listening requirements of a simple task or activity for a limited period.

Some students may find it difficult to cope with even a short duration activity where they are responsible for maintaining the conversation and flow of work. For such students, it may be necessary for a teacher to assist with the task. This will provide an important role model for students, as well as ensuring the task is completed.

Research and extension activities

This section gives students the chance to extend their developing English skills through short projects or tasks where they need to apply their knowledge. Students may need to travel to venues in the community such as to a local supermarket, in order to complete their research or extension project. This provides an ideal opportunity to extend students' skills so that they can travel independently or with limited assistance. They can also begin to learn about community venues which are relevant for their adult lives. These might include places such as job support agencies, Centrelink, workplaces, shopping centres and restaurants.

As with Book 1, the research and extension activities provide teachers with a chance to promote the fact that students are achieving success at a level which means they are ready to be 'extended'. For some students, who have heard more about failure than success, the simple use of the word 'extension' can be a powerful motivator for continued learning.

The importance of life skills

In Book 1, teachers were introduced to the important area of life skills. In Book 2, the life skills topics are aimed at young people who are getting ready for or already beginning their adult lives. They include areas which are important for interpersonal as well as work-based relationships and skills. Some of the life skills included in Book 2 are:

- **Personal care skills** – students learn about personal care and hygiene, with a focus on dressing for work or a job interview. They also learn about the personal care skills which are important in relationships.
- **Community skills** – students learn about the wider community, particularly in relation to finding work, participating in recreation activities and locating useful resources and facilities in their own area.
- **Social / interpersonal skills** – students learn about the social interactions that are expected of them as adults. Students need to be able to interact effectively with employers, real-estate agents, government agencies, friends, partners and family. The requirements of each of these relationships are different, and students need to be able to modify their language and behaviour accordingly.
- **Household skills** – this becomes a particularly important area for students as they get older. They need to be able to function as an adult member of a household effectively and safely, and to have an understanding of the literacy and language associated with

daily household activities. They need to know that the expectations of adults living independently are different from those of a child or teenager living at home. They also need to be able to access community services and support that can help them to maintain their living situations.

Guide to themes and life skills activities

This table provides a guide to some of the central themes and important life skills which are included in each unit of work.

Unit	Themes	Life skills
Pak and Jimmy's Place	Relationships Friendship Independence Working Managing a household	Organising daily activities Shopping Household tasks Managing problems Setting up a house Food preparation Hygiene
First Impressions	Body image Creating an impression Falling in love Attraction	Conversation skills Exercise and health Writing skills for work Creating an impression Choosing clothes Personal care
Out of Work	Finding employment Resources and support services Success and failure Confidence	Job-seeking skills Writing skills for work Resumes Recreation activities Further study Payments and benefits
Moving Out	Relationships Independence Family dynamics Cultural differences Moving out of home Parental expectations	Household appliances Household safety Following instructions Real-estate language The cost of moving out Setting up house Gender differences

Unit 1: Pak and Jimmy's Place

Before reading the story

Pre-reading activities are useful for all students before beginning a new unit of work. Activities such as these will help teachers establish the level of student understanding of basic concepts in the story, and give students a framework for topics to be covered during the unit.

1. Discuss words that students will encounter in the story, and check that they are familiar with their meanings. Words to check might include:

    - days of the week
    - carer
    - DVD / video
    - girlfriend
    - indoor cricket
    - kitchen / lounge room / bathroom
    - shopping

2. Talk about activities of daily living, and have students brainstorm a list of tasks or single words which can then be divided into categories. Categories might include:

    - meals
    - shopping
    - personal care
    - housework and cleaning
    - money
    - transport
    - work

3. Ask students to draw a picture or write a paragraph describing their ideal first home. They should include information such as who would be living in it, what the garden would be like, where the house would be located and how many rooms would be in it.

4. Discuss services that are available to help people with disabilities to live independently in the community. Ask students to suggest why these services are important, and what might happen if they were not available. Try to promote the idea that people with disabilities are capable, independent people who can make choices about the services they require. Avoid stereotypes such as the disabled person as a victim who 'suffers' from a disability.

 Literacy for Living: Book 2 (Phoenix Education) © Anne Vize 2003

About the story

Pak and Jimmy have just started sharing a house together. They are both excited to finally be living independently. They enjoy doing all the things that most young adults do when they move out on their own. Pak works as a cleaner and Jimmy works on a recycling program at a local centre. They go shopping for their groceries at the supermarket. They invite friends over for pizza on Friday nights. They watch DVDs and listen to music.

Pak understands that Jimmy needs a bit more help to do things than he does. Jimmy can be a bit forgetful and he has trouble remembering where he has put things sometimes. Pak just wishes he didn't always have to be the one to do all the putting away and cleaning up jobs! Pak enjoys spending time with his girlfriend, Sarah. Sarah is a fitness nut and Pak wishes she would relax a bit about how she looks. Jimmy enjoys playing indoor cricket with his friends and going out on weekends. He secretly wishes he had a girlfriend like Sarah to spend time with.

Read **Pak and Jimmy's Place** and find out what they both do during the week.

- Practise some of the days of the week.

- Learn about the world of work.

- Find out about going shopping.

- See what the record is for eating pizza.

- Find out why Jimmy spends so much money on videos.

- Discover why Pak sometimes has a cold shower.

- See who should never be left in charge of a shopping trolley.

Pak and Jimmy's Place

Pak and Jimmy have just moved in to a shared house in Chelsea. They both had to wait several years for their names to come up on the housing list, so they are very excited to finally be in their own place. Although it is fairly small, they love living there because they can walk to the end of their street and be standing on the beach. They have a bedroom each, and at the moment there is one spare room. There is a kitchen in the middle of the house, and a lounge room with a television and a DVD player. This is Jimmy's favourite room. He loves to sit in his old armchair and watch the DVDs that he buys from Cash Converters. He has seen some great movies, although sometimes the cheaper ones don't work very well and stop halfway through. When this happens, he has to hire the movie on video so he can see how it ends. He hates not knowing how a movie finishes! Pak always laughs when this happens, and tells him he should just hire the videos in the first place, and save himself some money.

The rules of the house say that they are meant to share all the chores, but sometimes Pak thinks he does more than his fair share. Each morning, Pak gets breakfast ready while Jimmy has his shower. He lays out the breakfast things on the bench. Cereal, milk, fruit juice, bread, margarine and jam are up one end of the bench. Bowls, plates and glasses are down the other end. He boils the kettle for his coffee and makes a Milo for Jimmy. Sometimes, if Jimmy is taking too long, he fills the kettle while he can still hear the water running in the shower. The yell from the bathroom when the water suddenly goes cold always makes him laugh. It seems like Jimmy will never learn to have a quick shower.

When Jimmy finally comes out of the bathroom, they sit together in the kitchen to eat their breakfast. Then, if Jimmy has left him any hot water, Pak has his shower while Jimmy cleans the kitchen. Mostly this means that Pak has a cold shower and then comes back to the kitchen to finish putting away all the things that Jimmy has forgotten. He doesn't really mind doing this, because he knows that Jimmy has trouble remembering where everything goes. Sometimes he thinks that Jimmy's memory has a deliberately forgetful switch inside it, especially when he finds that nothing has been put away at all and Jimmy is happily sitting in the lounge room watching the TV.

On weekdays, Jimmy and Pak both have to make sure they are ready to leave the house at 7.45 am sharp. Jimmy checks he has enough money for his weekly ticket, and Pak checks that all the windows and doors are locked and the lights are turned out. They both catch the bus from the corner of their street. Pak goes to his cleaning job and Jimmy goes to work on the recycling program at a local centre. For the last few weeks, they have been meeting a woman called Amanda on the bus. She has been helping Pak to learn how to work on his own as a cleaner at the factory. Pak thinks that soon he will be ready to do his job without Amanda to help him, although he stills finds it hard to remember the names of all the different chemicals that he has to use.

The bus stops at the centre first for Jimmy to get off. Some mornings, Jimmy gets distracted listening to his headphones and forgets where they are. He is still singing in his loud off-key voice when the bus pulls in to the driveway. If Pak didn't prod him with his elbow and point out the window, Jimmy would probably sit there all day, singing and drumming on the back of the seat with his fingers.

On Tuesdays, Jimmy and Pak go shopping with a carer at the local supermarket. The carer helps them to plan their meals for the week, and work out how much they can afford to spend. Next to watching his DVDs, shopping is Jimmy's favourite activity. The carer and Pak have to watch him closely to make sure there are not too many extras that get slipped into the trolley as they walk around the store. If they let Jimmy do the shopping, they would end up with a trolley full of ice-creams, biscuits and chocolate bars, and no vegetables at all. When they get home, the carer helps them organise the pantry and fridge so they can find everything they need for each meal. She makes sure the meat is labelled and put in the freezer, and that all the fruit and vegetables have been washed. She helps them write a list of what they are going to cook for each meal, and which ingredients they will need.

On Wednesdays, Jimmy plays indoor cricket after work. He has been playing for years, and next to watching DVDs and shopping, it is his favourite activity. This year he has been made captain of the team, and he takes his job very seriously. He always makes sure he is there at least fifteen minutes before game time to check that everything is ready. There is a lot to do. Score sheets have to be organised, and he needs to check which team they are playing. He makes sure everyone in the team does a warm-up and some stretches before they play so there are no injuries. After the game is over, he makes sure they shake hands with the players from the other team, and thank them for the game. Sometimes they stay and watch some of the other teams at the sports centre. Jimmy likes to watch the basketball, but some of the other guys prefer to watch the women's volleyball that is on at the same time. Jimmy doubts that it is really the volleyball game itself that the guys are interested in!

On Friday nights, Jimmy and Pak often invite some friends over for pizza. They both love ham and pineapple pizza. The record for the most number of slices eaten in one night is nine, and is held by Pak. Jimmy has had many tries at beating the record, but so far he has only managed six slices before starting to feel sick. Pak knows that as long as Jimmy keeps eating a whole garlic bread roll on his own before starting on the pizza, his record is safe. Pak's girlfriend, Sarah, always tells them they are revolting for eating so much pizza. She usually has a salad and some fresh fruit on pizza nights because she says she is watching her weight. Neither Pak nor Jimmy can understand this, because Sarah is tall and slender, with a tiny waist that fits neatly into her blue jeans. But they figure that so long as Sarah is happy to watch her weight and eat salad, they are happy to watch the television and eat pizza!

On weekends, both Jimmy and Pak like to sleep in. They usually wake up around ten, and have a slow, lazy breakfast of bacon and eggs while they read the paper. Pak reads the news while Jimmy looks through the sports section and TV guide. After breakfast, Pak goes to the pool to swim with Sarah. She swims freestyle up and down the pool, counting her laps at each end. Pak does a few laps, then splashes around in the shallow end and watches her swim. Sarah keeps telling him there is no point going to the pool if he is not going to work on his fitness. Pak tells her that his fitness is fine on its own, and besides, it is important that she has a coach and he is happy to be it. Pak enjoys these trips to the pool, because he gets to spend time with Sarah without having to worry about what Jimmy is doing.

Jimmy has a carer who arrives around lunchtime on Saturdays to take him out. If it is fine they might go to the park near their house to kick a footy. If it is raining they catch the train into the city to see a movie. In summer they take their fishing rods to the beach at Mordialloc to see if the flathead are biting. Jimmy looks forward to these days out. He likes doing his own thing without having Pak tell him what to do all the time.

On Sundays, Jimmy goes to visit his mum at her flat in Glen Iris. He walks to the train station, then catches a train and a tram. The whole trip takes him about an hour and a half. He finds it relaxing to sit in the carriage as the train sways from side to side and the houses flash past the window. Pak usually spends Sundays with Sarah. He calls in to pick her up at her house, and they either go out for lunch or walk along the beach. This is their special time, when no one interrupts them and neither of them has to be anywhere else.

On Sunday nights, Sarah's mum often invites Pak to stay for dinner. Sarah's mum cooks a roast dinner every Sunday, and the whole family sit at the table together and talk about what they have done over the weekend. Pak sometimes feels sorry for Jimmy on Sunday nights. Jimmy does not have a girlfriend to spend time with on weekends. Pak knows that sometimes Jimmy gets lonely. If he remembers, he picks up a chocolate bar or an ice-cream from the milkbar near their house as he is on his way home. He knows that Jimmy will have cooked himself cheese on toast or scrambled eggs for dinner, and will be sitting in his favourite chair watching the TV. It always makes him laugh that Jimmy can get so excited about one little chocolate or ice-cream – it reminds him of a little kid getting a present.

On Sunday nights they both like to check that they have everything ready for the week. This is more Pak's habit than Jimmy's. On his own, Jimmy would start the week with his usual panic, trying to find clothes, keys and wallet. But Pak is gradually helping Jimmy to realise that if he lays his clothes out ready for the morning with his keys and wallet next to the bed, it makes the start of the week a whole lot easier. They are both usually in bed by about ten o'clock on Sundays. Pak reads his book in bed for a while before he falls asleep, and Jimmy listens to the radio. By Monday morning they are both feeling fresh and ready for the new week.

Activity suggestions for beginning readers

These activities will be useful for students who have limited reading skills, and who will prefer to listen to the story rather than read it independently. The activities cover a range of presentation types in order to cater for a variety of preferred student learning styles. The use of concrete objects can help students to retain information presented during these activities, and can be used as a way of teaching key words from the story.

1. **Job support agency** – Visit a local job support agency or ask a speaker from an agency to talk to students about the services that are available. Make sure you take notes yourself so that you can reinforce any important details which may have been missed by students during the talk.

2. **Public transport** – Take students on trips using public transport to various local centres of employment. Talk about the sorts of jobs that are available in different areas and how students would need to plan their trips to and from work. Some examples to cover with students might include:

   - Shopping centres (retail industry, food service, cleaning)
   - Hotels/motels (cleaning, food service, hospitality, customer service)
   - Light industry (factory work, automotive, food processing, clothing production)
   - Heavy industry (building, construction, larger manufacturing plants)
   - Supported employment programs (gardening, recycling, manufacturing, packing, retail services, one to one support in open employment)

3. **Work safety** – Discuss what safety at work means and ask students to think of examples of risks at a variety of workplaces. It may also be helpful to give students strategies they could use if they felt they were in an unsafe situation.

4. **Transition to work** – Discuss how students feel about making a transition from a training or schooling environment into a workplace. Often students feel anxious that their social networks and security will be disrupted or lost completely and that they may be heading for a place where they will feel isolated, confused and at risk. Strategies to suggest might include:

   - Regular social activities organised with current friendship groups before making a transition to a workplace
   - Using an address book with names, addresses and phone numbers
   - Establishing a sports team of current friends
   - Setting up a buddy system for students at a new workplace
   - Talking about fears and concerns with someone trusted, for example a teacher, friend, family member or staff member from an agency or support service
   - Doing work experience for a short period before making a complete transition to work

5. **Setting up a kitchen** – Bring in a number of actual kitchen utensils or photographs of utensils and ask students to name each one and talk about what they are used for. Divide the objects or photos into piles of essential and non-essential items, and talk about whether any could be used in place of each other. (For example, grilling toast instead of using a toaster.)

6. **Pricing kitchen items** – Visit a shopping centre or use catalogues to make a poster of the cost of various kitchen items. Check that students have an understanding of relative values of items, and how prices can vary from one shop to another and from one brand to another.

7. **Problem solving** – Ask students to work in pairs or small groups to solve a variety of household problems. These can be written or drawn onto cards or explained verbally. Examples might include:

   - A housemate not doing their fair share of the housework
   - Hearing scary noises at night
   - Being burgled
   - Having a problem or dispute with a neighbour
   - Not owning a lawn mower and needing to cut the grass
   - Moving into a new area and not knowing where local shops and services are located
   - A housemate inviting too many friends around all the time
   - Not having enough room to put all your belongings

8. **Housework tasks** – Have students make a poster of housework tasks for each room of the house, and add information about equipment needed, precautions and frequency for each task.

9. **Things you need to know** – Run a session for students on some of life's essentials that they have possibly never been shown. These might include:

   - Changing a bag in a vacuum cleaner
   - Changing batteries in an alarm clock or smoke detector
   - Tightening a screw with a screwdriver
   - Getting the lid off a jar when it is stuck
   - Changing a light globe
   - Turning the power to the house on or off
   - Turning the water to the house on or off
   - Emptying the lint filter in a washing machine and/or dryer
   - Dividing clothes into 'coloured' and 'non-coloured' piles for washing
   - Finding a leak in an air mattress
   - Microwaving a container with a metal lid
   - Checking if the milk is still safe to drink

Matching words

Use a line to match each of these word endings with their correct beginning. There is an example to help you get started. Next, copy out the words on the list and use five of them in a short paragraph.

sal	end
troll	ow
piz	times
differ	fast
al	friend
shall	ing
win	za
some	ad
aff	dow
girl	ord
show	ey
break	ent
cer	ways
week	eal

_____
_____
_____
_____
_____
_____
_____

Missing letters

Fill in the missing letters using the clues to help you. An example has been done to show you.

Example

W _e_ _e_ **k**   There are 7 days in one of these

1.	M _ _ _ ay	First day of the working week
2.	_ _ _ day	Last day of the working week
3.	Sw _ _	You do this in a pool
4.	Break _ _ _ _	The first meal of the day
5.	Sal _ _	A healthy food
6.	Tr _ _ n	A type of transport
7.	Wa _ _ et	A place to keep money
8.	Lone _ _	On your own too much
9.	_ _ sh	Doing something quickly
10.	Scram _ _ _ _	A way of cooking eggs
11.	Morn _ _ _	The first part of the day
12.	_ _ _ ourite	You like it a lot
13.	Ke _ _ le	Use this to boil water
14.	Bedr _ _ m	Room where you sleep
15.	Tro _ _ ey	Use this when you go shopping
16.	Ba _ _ room	Room where you clean your teeth
17.	Ch _ _ _ lat _	Don't eat too much of this!

Alphabetical order

These sets of words are from the story **Pak and Jimmy's Place**. Put each set into alphabetical order. As an extra challenge, see if you can write a sentence that contains all the words from one set.

1. although, eat, cheaper, deal, favourite, both

_____

_____

2. kitchen, bathroom, bedroom, lounge room, toilet, laundry

_____

_____

3. video, television, movie, football, swim, fishing

_____

_____

4. bacon, jam, milk, toast, egg, cereal

_____

_____

5. bread, coffee, margarine, cereal, bacon, milk

_____

_____

6. shower, share, sometimes, street, so, save

_____

_____

7. there, the, then, this, that, they

_____

_____

8. work, week, pizza, pineapple, swim, splash

_____

_____

_____

_____

What does it mean?

Use a dictionary or write your own definitions for each of these words from **Pak and Jimmy's Place**.

1. Spare _____

_____

2. Cheap _____

_____

3. Forgotten _____

_____

4. Deliberate _____

_____

5. Team _____

_____

6. Distracted _____

_____

7. Favourite _____

_____

8. Careful _____

_____

9. Organise _____

_____

10. Lazy _____

_____

11. Lonely _____

_____

12. Recycling _____

_____

13. Indoor cricket _____

_____

Change the meaning

The groups of letters we put on the end of words are called suffixes. **'ing'** is a suffix that can be added to the end of a word to change its meaning. Add an 'ing' to each of these words to make a new word.

Hint! Take away the 'e' if there is one on the end of the word, before you add the 'ing'.

1. Tell   _____

2. Read   _____

3. Walk   _____

4. Live   _____

5. Visit   _____

6. Share   _____

7. Hire   _____

8. Eat   _____

9. Shower   _____

10. Make   _____

11. Invite   _____

12. Remember   _____

13. Work   _____

A challenge!

When you have finished, choose eight of the words from the list and use them in a single sentence.

_____

_____

_____

_____

The great shopping challenge!

Jimmy thinks he can do the weekly shopping for less than Pak. Pak is sure he will beat Jimmy at this challenge! Use a calculator to add up both lists and see who won. Now, read the lists again and check that you know all the words. Use your usual word-solving strategies for this task (sound the letters out, look for letter combinations you recognise, or ask someone to help you).

PAK		JIMMY	
2 litres of orange juice	$4.15	6 cans of soft drink	$4.85
1 box of cereal	$4.90	1 pack of chocolate biscuits	$3.50
1 packet of flour	$1.20	6 small flavoured milk drinks	$3.78
1 litre of milk	$1.70	1 heat and eat pizza	$4.29
6 bananas	$2.78	2 frozen meat pies (small)	$3.25
6 apples	$2.22	1 tin of peaches	$1.90
1 tin of strawberry jam	$2.79	1 bottle of pasta sauce	$3.90
1 loaf of wholemeal bread	$2.00	1 magazine	$2.80
1 tin of baked beans	$1.02	2 packets of rice noodle snacks	$2.20
1 dozen eggs	$2.99	4 cheese dips	$3.40
1 tub of margarine	$2.79	6 flavoured muesli bars	$4.15
1 bunch of celery	$1.20	1 tin of noodle soup	$1.60
3 tomatoes	$0.95	1 jar of pancake mix	$3.79
half a watermelon	$1.10	2 flavoured yoghurts	$1.78
TOTAL		TOTAL	

Name:

True or false?

Circle true or false for each of these sentences about the story. You may need to look back at the story for some of your answers.

1.	Pak and Jimmy catch the train to work.	TRUE	FALSE
2.	Jimmy likes to watch DVDs.	TRUE	FALSE
3.	Pak's girlfriend is Sandra.	TRUE	FALSE
4.	Jimmy's mum lives in Mordialloc.	TRUE	FALSE
5.	Sometimes Jimmy goes fishing.	TRUE	FALSE
6.	Jimmy listens to music on the bus.	TRUE	FALSE
7.	Pak works as a cleaner.	TRUE	FALSE
8.	Amanda is helping Pak at work.	TRUE	FALSE
9.	Jimmy plays indoor cricket.	TRUE	FALSE
10.	Sarah likes to go swimming.	TRUE	FALSE
11.	Pak and Sarah live together.	TRUE	FALSE
12.	Jimmy's mum lives in Glen Iris.	TRUE	FALSE
13.	Pak and Jimmy live in Chelsea.	TRUE	FALSE

How well did you read?

Answer these questions about **Pak and Jimmy's Place**. You may need to go back and read some of the story again to get all your answers.

1. Who gets breakfast ready?

_____

2. Who sometimes has a cold shower?

_____

3. In which suburb is Pak and Jimmy's house?

_____

4. Is there a spare room in the house?

_____

5. Who drinks Milo for breakfast?

_____

6. What time do Pak and Jimmy leave the house on a weekday?

_____

7. Who helps Pak at work?

_____

8. What night of the week is pizza night?

_____

How should it look?

Use information from the story to help you draw a picture of each of these.

Breakfast time	Going shopping
At the cricket game	Pizza night

Finish the sentence!

Use these sentence starters to help you write your own sentences about Pak and Jimmy. When you have finished, swap your work with a partner and give each other some feedback.

1.   Pak laughs when Jimmy …

2.   Jimmy likes to …

3.   Sarah thinks that …

4.   When they are shopping …

5.   Pak and Jimmy catch the bus …

6.   On Fridays …

7.   Pak and Sarah go …

8.   Jimmy and his carer …

9.   The record for pizza eating …

10.   Pak sometimes worries that …

11.   Pak helps Jimmy to …

12.   On Sunday nights …

Budgeting

Pak and Jimmy want to go on a holiday next year. Here are their weekly budgets. Estimate how much they might spend on weekly bills and other costs. Then decide how much they can both save towards their holiday during one year.

PAK: income = $270 per week

Weekly expenses	Amount
Rent	$80
Savings per week	
Savings in one year	

JIMMY: income = $255 per week

Weekly expenses	Amount
Rent	$80
Savings per week	
Savings in one year	

Moving out of home

What skills do you need?

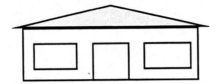

Moving out of home is an exciting time, but it is also a time when you need to learn lots of new skills. For each of the areas below, list the skills or tasks you think are important.

Then, choose a skill from your list that you can't already do. Write it in the box below, and then write down how you could learn to do it.

Shopping

Important skills:

1. eg *Make a shopping list before going to the shops*

2.

3.

4.

A skill I need to learn is: _____

How I could do this:

continued ...

Moving out of home – what skills do you need?

Housework

Important skills:

1.

2.

3.

4.

A skill I need to learn is: _____

How I could do this:

Budgeting / managing money

Important skills:

1.

2.

3.

4.

A skill I need to learn is: _____

How I could do this:

continued ...

Moving out of home – what skills do you need?

Getting along with others

Important skills:

1.

2.

3.

4.

A skill I need to learn is: _____

How I could do this:

Cooking / preparing meals

Important skills:

1.

2.

3.

4.

A skill I need to learn is: _____

How I could do this:

continued ...

Moving out of home – what skills do you need?

Personal care (showering, make-up etc)

Important skills:

1.

2.

3.

4.

A skill I need to learn is: _____

How I could do this:

Clothes (choosing, buying, looking after)

Important skills:

1.

2.

3.

4.

A skill I need to learn is: _____

How I could do this:

continued ...

Moving out of home – what skills do you need?

Travel / transport

Important skills:

1.

2.

3.

4.

A skill I need to learn is: _____

How I could do this:

Entertaining

Important skills:

1.

2.

3.

4.

A skill I need to learn is: _____

How I could do this:

Setting up rooms

For each of the rooms below, list or draw some of the items you would need to have when you move into a new house. There are a few suggestions to get you started.

KITCHEN

frying pan

BATHROOM

deodorant

BEDROOM

doona cover

LAUNDRY

washing machine

Housemate needed

Someone new is going to move in with Pak and Jimmy. They don't want just any old housemate, they are looking for someone special. Help them design the ultimate housemate, complete with labels showing all the great things they can do!

Solving problems – making decisions

Work with your group to find the best solutions to each of the given problems. There may not always be a perfect fix, but try to weigh up the alternatives to come up with the best option. Use this step-by-step plan to help you think through each problem.

PROBLEM

What is the main problem to be solved?

OPTIONS

Think of all the possible solutions to the problem – don't rule anything out yet!

EVALUATE

Wait a while and see if you are still happy with your decision. If not, go back to the first step and start again!

PLUSES
Think of all the pluses for each option.

MINUSES
Think of all the minuses for each option

BEST OPTION

Decide on the best option after you have weighed up the pluses and minuses of each one.

continued ...

Problem 1: Break in?

You arrive home to find the front door is already open. You cannot hear any noises from inside the house and no one answers when you call out from the doorway. You were not expecting anyone to be at home.

What do you do?

Problem 2 : Frequent visitor

Your housemate has been inviting his girlfriend over most nights during the week. They stay up late listening to music that keeps you awake. You like his girlfriend and would like to stay friends with both of them, but you are getting tired of her being around so much.

What do you do?

Problem 3: Budget blow out

You have blown the weekly budget on junk food and a day out in the city, and you remember that you have invited a group of friends around for dinner on Saturday night. You only have $20 left to provide dinner for six people.

What do you do?

continued ...

Problem 4: Constant arguments

You and your housemates are arguing constantly about everything from the amount of time you spend in the shower to who does the dishes and puts the rubbish out. You cannot have a conversation without it ending in a disagreement.

What do you do?

Problem 5: Lease problems

Your landlord has written you a letter saying that he has decided to sell the house and that you will have to move out in about four weeks. You have signed a lease for the next three months, but you do not know if you should ask to be able to stay until the lease is finished, or just do what the landlord wants. You find it hard to write letters to people because your spelling is not very good.

What do you do?

Problem 6: To interfere or not?

The couple who live next door to you fight all the time. You can hear them yelling at each other late at night, and sometimes it sounds as if someone is being hurt. You are scared of the husband but you feel sorry for his wife. You are not sure if you should interfere or not.

What do you do?

Housework tasks

Work with a partner to think of 5 housework tasks that need to be done for each of these rooms. Then estimate the time it would take to finish each task and add up the total housework times for each room, and for the house as a whole.

Housework times

Bedroom	**Bathroom**
Lounge room	**Kitchen**

Bedroom   _____

Bathroom   _____

Lounge room   _____

Kitchen   _____

Total housework time   _____

Discussion topics

Choose a topic to discuss, then present your ideas to the class. You may like to work with a partner for this activity.

You need to interview a new housemate to share your house. What do you need to find out about him or her?

What can you do to make your house safe from fire?

How do you plan for a special event or celebration?

What can you to make your house safe from burglars?

What are your rights as a tenant?

How do you plan a great (and safe) party in your new house?

How do you run a house meeting? Why are they important? What do you talk about?

Poems

Work with a partner to make up a poem on one of these topics. Use each of the letters from the word as the start of each line of your poem. Your poem does not need to rhyme. Read your poem out loud to the group when it is finished.

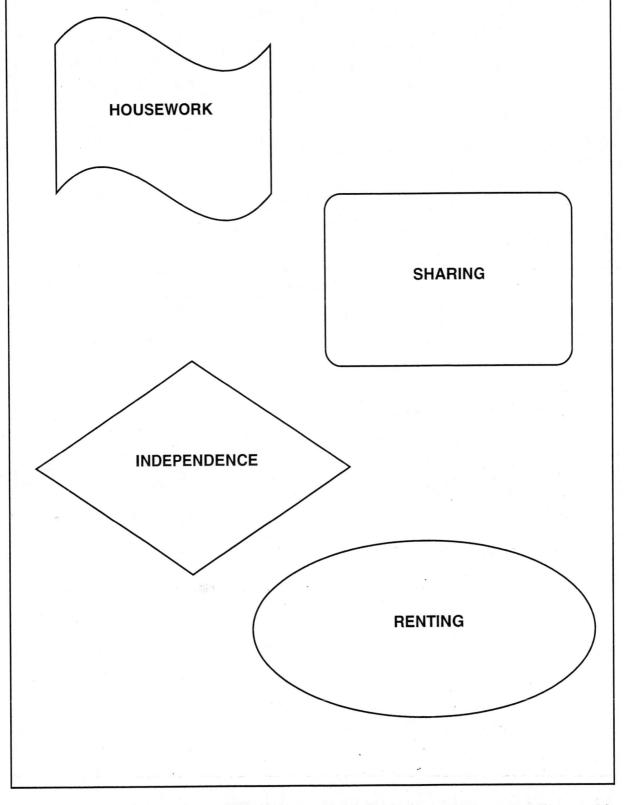

HOUSEWORK

SHARING

INDEPENDENCE

RENTING

How do you cook that?

Here are a number of meals that are quick and easy to prepare. Research the ingredients, equipment and method for one of these meals.

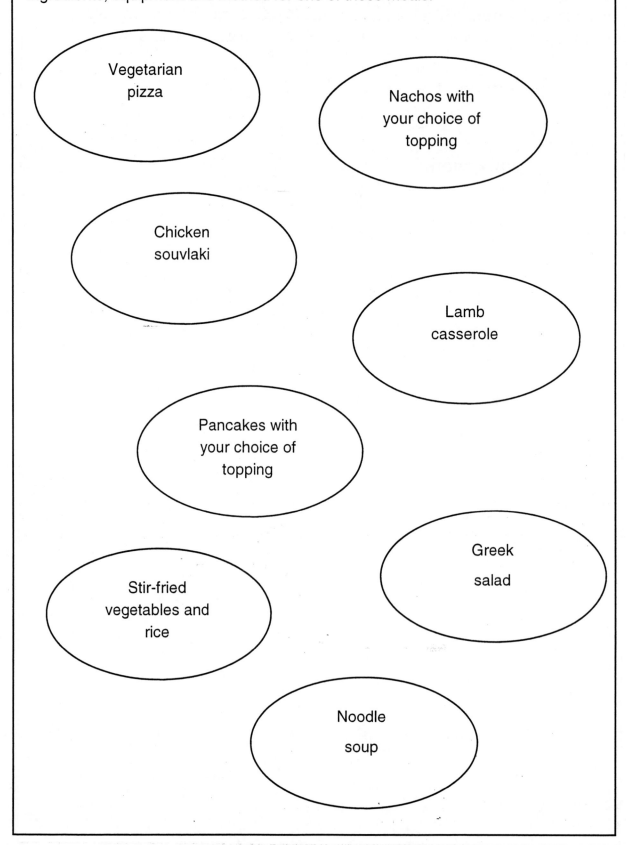

Housework – how often do you do it?

S	M	T	W	Th	F	S

Draw up a table with 3 columns – headed 'Daily, 'Weekly' and 'Occasionally'.

For each of the tasks below, decide how often they should be done and write them into the correct column of your table.

shop for groceries	pay the electricity bill
sweep the floor	wash the dishes
wash clothes	wash the windows
change sheets and pillow cases	clean the shower
check smoke detector battery	turn lights off
turn heater off	check front door is locked
put dirty clothes in laundry basket	vacuum carpet
empty dishwasher	clean kitchen benches
hang up towel in bathroom	pick up clothes from floor
iron clothes	dust window sills
empty kitchen bin	put out recycling
walk the dog	water the garden
mow the grass	cook the dinner
check answering machine	wash the car

Now look back at the lists you have made. Put a tick (✔) next to all the tasks you can do yourself. Rule a line through any jobs that you think *never* need to be done.

Setting up a kitchen – what does it cost?

Find a price in a catalogue for each of these items, and then add them up to get a total cost. With a partner or in a small group, think of some ideas for setting up your kitchen on a budget.

ITEM	COST
vegetable peeler	
grater	
strainer / colander	
measuring cups	
wooden spoon	
sharp knife	
mixing bowl	
tongs	
plastic jug	
chopping board	
frying pan	
set of saucepans	
Total	

Ideas for setting up a kitchen on a budget:

1.

2.

3.

4.

Getting there on time

Imagine that you have a job where you start at 8.00 am. Your bus trip takes **20 minutes**, and it takes **5 minutes** to walk to the bus stop. Use the list of tasks below to plan your morning routine. Estimate how long each task takes, and then work out what time you need to get up so you are at work by 8.00 am.

clean teeth	shower	get dressed
find clothes	prepare breakfast	eat breakfast
brush hair	make lunch	pack bag
secure house	shave	pack away breakfast
find keys and wallet	get out of bed	wash hair
iron shirt	walk to bus	bus trip

TASK	TIME ALLOWED	TIME TO START

Job support agencies

Use your research skills to find out the answers to these questions about two job support agencies in your local area. You may need to use a phone book, read brochures or make some phone calls. Write your answers in the spaces provided.

Agency 1

Agency name _____

Agency address _____

_____

Agency phone number _____

Name of a contact person _____

Who will they work with? _____

Are there any costs? _____

What sorts of jobs will they help you look for? _____

_____

_____

Agency 2

Agency name _____

Agency address _____

_____

Agency phone number _____

Name of a contact person _____

Who will they work with? _____

Are there any costs? _____

What sorts of jobs will they help you look for? _____

_____

_____

Unit 1 Pak and Jimmy's Place: Learning checklist **Name:**

This checklist allows you to keep track of the worksheets and activities that you have agreed to complete with the help and support of your teacher. Once you have agreed on the activities you are going to do for this unit, you can use the checklist as a tool for remembering what you need to do and for keeping a record of your achievements.

Worksheet / activity	Tick if chosen	Date completed	Checked
1.2 Matching words			
1.3 Missing letters			
1.4 Alphabetical order			
1.5 What does it mean?			
1.6 Change the meaning			
1.7 The great shopping challenge			
1.8 True or false?			
1.9 How well did you read?			
1.10 How should it look?			
1.11 Finish the sentence			
1.12 Budgeting			
1.13 Moving out of home			
1.14 Setting up rooms			
1.15 Housemate needed			
1.16 Solving problems			
1.17 Housework tasks			
1.18 Discussion topics			
1.19 Poems			
1.20 How do you cook that?			
1.21 Housework – how often?			
1.22 Setting up a kitchen			
1.23 Getting there on time			
1.24 Job support agencies			

Unit 2: First Impressions

Before reading the story

Pre-reading activities are useful for all students before beginning a new unit of work. Activities such as these will help teachers establish the level of student understanding of basic concepts contained within the story, and give students a framework for topics to be covered during the unit.

1.   **Compare school and TAFE. What are the similarities and differences?**

Similarities: learning lots of different subjects, both have teachers and students, both are usually quite large places, both have classrooms, both usually have a cafeteria or canteen and a library, both have homework, both have rules about how you need to behave.

Differences: more freedom to do what you want at TAFE, schools have principals and TAFES do not, at TAFE you do not have to wear a school uniform, at TAFE you might have classes at night, at TAFE you are allowed to smoke, at TAFE you do not have a homeroom teacher.

2.   **What are some of the subjects can you study at TAFE ?**

Examples might include: automotive studies, hospitality, sport and recreation, horticulture, carpentry, childcare, hairdressing, wine-making, boat-building, welding, office studies, computing, photography, art and design.

3.   **Imagine you were trying to impress someone. What might you do and say to make a good impression? What would you try not to do?**

Discuss issues such as personal hygiene, choice of clothes, body language and spoken language with students. What are some of the things that impress students when they meet a new person and what do they find is a turn-off?

4.   **Draw a picture of your ideal boyfriend or girlfriend.**

Ask students to label their drawings or to tell you what it is that makes this person ideal. Encourage students to focus on personal qualities as well as physical attributes.

5.   **Make a list of some of the things people might do when they are boyfriend and girlfriend.**

Examples might include (adapt to suit age group): kissing, holding hands, cuddling, touching, sleeping together, sending flowers, sending Valentine cards, having romantic nights out, sharing a meal, going to the movies, going for walks, playing sport together, talking.

6   **Make a list of some of the things people might do when they are friends.**

Examples might include: sharing a meal, playing sport, mucking around, going to the beach, going to the movies, talking.

7. **What can you do if you like someone but they don't like you?**

Discussion points to consider might include whether you are compatible with the person, why you think they don't like you, appropriate social behaviour, and dealing with rejection in an adult way. It is important to make sure students do not hold the belief that they have the right to force anyone to be in a relationship or to do anything against their will.

Before you read

Sometimes in life it is good to be able to laugh at yourself. Occasionally it is also good fun to be able to laugh at other people. This story gives you that chance!

It is a story about Frances, who falls in love with Brett. Frances is like most people – just average. She is fairly ordinary looking. She is good at sports, okay at school, and lousy at doing her own hair. Brett, on the other hand, is gorgeous, talented and great fun to be with. Everyone wants to be friends with Brett. But Frances decides she wants to be more than just friends. She wants Brett to fall in love with her. But before he can fall in love, he has to notice that she actually exists!

In **First Impressions**, you will enjoy reading about Frances's many attempts to attract Brett's attention. Unfortunately for Frances, not all her attempts to attract Brett's attention turn out quite the way she planned! You will find there is a surprising twist at the end of this story, as Frances and Brett both learn some valuable lessons about themselves and each other.

- Does Frances finally get her man?

- Is Brett really as good as everyone thinks?

- What is Brett's secret?

- Are looks the most important thing?

- What is the best way to let someone know that you like them?

- Do people really fall in love at first sight?

Read **First Impressions** and find out!

First Impressions

Brett is sixteen and one of the biggest attractions at our TAFE. He has wavy brown hair, blue eyes and a cute button nose. He is friends with everyone who matters. Wherever he goes, he is surrounded by an admiring group of people. He changes girlfriends as often as most people change their socks, and each one seems to be more gorgeous than the last. When he speaks, everyone listens, including me. My name is Frances. I am fifteen and I have just started at TAFE this year. I have straight red hair and freckles, and teeth that don't line up quite right in the middle. My single most important challenge for this year is to get Brett to notice me. I have decided that this will be my mission. I know I really should be spending my time concentrating in class and making sure I 'get the most out of my TAFE experience' (I think I read that in a handbook somewhere). But I have decided that you only get one chance at real, true, trip-you-over and make-your-head-spin type love. And this is it. Brett. Just the way his name sounds makes my ears tingle. I lie awake at night whispering to myself 'Brett, Brett, Brett', until my sister throws pillows at me and threatens to tell Mum.

I have my own group of friends at TAFE. There is Linh, who went to school with me last year. We have been friends for ages, and I tell her everything. There is Tamiko, who I have just met a few months ago. She is younger than Linh and me, and is forever getting into trouble. This is mostly because she can't remember to keep her mouth shut and has an opinion on everything. Linh and I have started sitting one each side of her so we can elbow her when she is about to say the wrong thing in class. And there is Henri, who hangs around with us because no one else will put up with him. He has a funny stutter when he speaks, and he smells a bit strange, but he is okay when you get to know him. He came to TAFE from a school in the country where all the other kids used to pick on him something fierce. He has told us a few horror stories about having his head flushed and glue poured into his pencil case and things like that. His stutter gets worse when he talks to anyone except us. I guess that is why he spends so much time with us – we can do the talking for him, and he can just stand there. He seems to like that.

I actually started my 'Brett – notice me' mission yesterday, and I have to admit that so far things are not going as well as I had hoped. In class last week, one of our teachers was telling us about the importance of first impressions. We talked about how to dress for a job interview, and how to dress if you want someone special to notice you. We also talked about make-up and shaving and choosing clothes to suit your body shape and special features. I think that was a nice way of saying if you are a beanpole already, stripes should not be your first choice, and if you are drop dead gorgeous, you can wear anything you like. So I decided it was time to give up the tracksuit pants and footy beanie, and make a serious impression.

I set my alarm for 6.30 am so I would have enough time to get ready. I showered, then took my sister's hairdryer out of the drawer. I am what you could safely call a hairdryer novice, but I wasn't too disappointed with the end result. A bit frizzy maybe, but otherwise okay. I put on a little more make-up than usual, and apart from a few blodgy bits around my eyes, I think I did quite well. My cheeks were dusted a soft pink, and my eyelashes stood out starkly with mascara. I had to force myself not to blink because my eyes kept sticking closed when I did. I searched through my sister's wardrobe for the long black skirt that I knew she had lurking in there somewhere. I teamed this with my own best shirt and my only pair of high heels. I grabbed a quick piece of toast and a Milo for breakfast and raced out the door for the bus.

Now you might think that all this effort would have been rewarded by an admiring glance or a polite comment from the chosen love of my life. After all, a lot of time and thought had gone into the impression I had created for Brett's benefit. Well …

By the time I arrived at the bus stop, my feet were aching from the high heels and I could feel little beads of sweat trickling down my back. I leapt onto the bus just before it pulled out from the stop, earning myself a few harsh words from the bus driver about not leaving everything to the last minute. The seat I found up the back had chewing gum stuck to it, which of course stuck to my skirt. I spent most of the bus trip with my skirt pulled around back to front trying to scrape the chewing gum off with an ice cream stick. A group of kids sitting in front of me had all the bus windows open. The wind blew through the bus so hard I ended up with all my hair pushed over to one side like a bird's nest about to fall out of its tree.

All this was forgotten when I arrived at TAFE and saw Brett standing at the entrance to our building. He was leaning casually against the wall talking to a few friends. He glanced up as I approached, my high heels tap-tap-tapping on the path. Just as I reached him, I stumbled on a stone and fell over. I stretched my arms out, and landed neatly amongst the cigarette butts at his feet. My skirt was up around my waist and my knickers were on plain view.

I was so embarrassed! I prayed hard for the earth to open up and swallow me whole. (The earth, of course, stayed just where it was.) The two girls standing with Brett started to giggle. Brett himself didn't seem at all bothered by the spectacle I had created. He reached out to where I was sitting on the ground and offered me his hand. As he helped my gently to my feet, he chuckled and said, 'Nice milk moustache you've got there!' I couldn't believe after all that, I had forgotten to wipe the Milo from my mouth!

** * * * * * * *

But today is barbecue day. My second chance to finish my mission. I am going to get Brett to notice me *and* be impressed by what he sees! First impressions are not everything, and there is always room for a second try. I have given up on the beautiful young woman look, and I am going to reinvent myself as a competent working girl. The barbecue today is the perfect chance.

We have been planning the barbecue in class for weeks. It is supposed to be a fundraiser for some charity or other, and a way of showing that we can all work as a team and get a job done. Until now, this has seemed like quite a tall order. As a group, we have all the motivation of Year 8s before a maths test. Our planning skills are barely enough to get a lunch order together, let alone run a barbecue. Ivan, our teacher, has been tearing his hair out trying to get us to join in and help so that he doesn't end up doing all the work himself. We have been trying to explain to him that he is the best person for the job because he has so much more experience in these things than we do. He must be better than us at planning big events. He has spent a lot of time lately saying that his doing all the work is hardly the idea of the class. He has also pointed out that if we don't get everything done we are going to look pretty silly standing in front of an empty barbecue with no gas trying to sell uncooked sausages on bread for a price we have yet to agree upon. I have to admit he has a point.

Tamiko has decided she is happy to join me as a competent working girl. We are sure that between us we can get the job done and look good at the same time. With both of us scribbling on notepads and shouting orders, it takes no time at all to set a price for the sausages, write a shopping list and organise the artwork for the posters. Our stunned classmates are set to work painting, collecting tables and shopping for bread and sausages. Ivan wonders what on earth has happened to his class. Soon the tables are set up in the courtyard, and the TAFE is decorated with posters. Some of the posters do read:

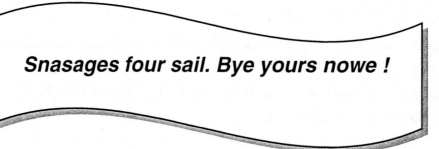

Snasages four sail. Bye yours nowe !

but at least everyone was involved.

A queue of people forms at the table, and we can tell from the muttering that they are starting to get impatient. Tamiko and I step in to get things moving along. Tamiko starts helping with the money and sorting out change, and I go to work at the sauce and mustard station. I can't believe my luck when I look up and see Brett next in line. He glances at me and I realise with relief that he has not recognised me as the clutz who fell all over him the day before. I toss my hair over my shoulder and carefully plan our conversation. It must sound chatty, but intelligent. Mature, but still fun to be with. Sensitive, but not dreamy. I take a deep breath.

'Would you like sauce with that?'

'Yeah, thanks,' he replies.

I take the sauce bottle from the table and point it at his sausage and bread. I try to think of something other than TAFE or weather to talk about. As I stand there, searching my brain for something clever to say, I follow his eyes down to the sauce bottle. Sauce is pouring out, covering the bread and now dripping onto the ground. Already a small red puddle has formed at his feet. My face blushes as red as the sauce, and I quickly shove a handful of paper towel at him. He shakes his head as he walks away, still wiping sauce from his arm. So much for being competent!

* * * * * * * *

I am not going to give up. Pre-schoolers give up. Primary kids give up. Teenagers always give up, mostly because they were never trying in the first place. But this is TAFE, and I am a different person. I am not going to give up on making a good impression. I think Brett and I have both got over the tomato sauce incident, although I don't think he will ever feel quite the same about barbecues or competent women. This afternoon is basketball, and if there is anything in this world at which I excel, it is basketball. I love the pounding of sneakers on sprung wooden floors, and the smack and swish as the ball hits the backboard then drops through the ring. I love running up and down the court, feeling my heart race and my muscles burn. I love jumping as high as I can and snatching the ball as it is in mid-flight.

The game this afternoon is between our class and another group. After a few stretches and a quick warm up, we start to play. The ball travels up and down the court, passing quickly between players. We are all good at basketball, and we enjoy playing hard. The two teams are evenly matched, and the scores are tied at the end of the first half. The whistle blows and we all collapse on the floor for a rest. A few people head outside for a smoke, while the rest of us take the chance to drink some water and chat while we recover. Brett walks into the gym just before the start of the second half. I see him stroll over to the teacher and talk to her, but I cannot hear what is said. He slides his bag across the floor, takes off his coat and joins the other team on the court. At last! Another chance to show Brett that I can be capable and attractive, and not just a clumsy girl who spills food everywhere.

We start to play again. With Brett's help, the other team is taking the lead. The score is now 26 to 20. Brett sinks a three-pointer, and brings the difference to nine points. I am panting from racing up and down the court, trying to cover every pass, doing anything I can to stop them scoring another goal. A gap opens up in front of me. I sprint forward just as Henri turns, looking for a free player. I call out to him and he grins as he sends the ball my way. I bounce it twice with my left hand, then switch to my right as I see another player coming towards me. I have the ring in my sights, and I plan my move in my head as I run. I take one final bounce, then jump. Out of the corner of my eye, I see an opposition player reaching for the ball. I hear a thud and feel a sharp pain shooting through my elbow. There is a sudden yell, and I look around to see a body lying on the court. The body groans and a hand slides around to feel the side of a bright red cheek. I realise to my horror that it is Brett. I have hit the man of my dreams in the head with my elbow!

I stand, red-faced, in the middle of the court, watching as the teacher gently puts ice on Brett's head. His team-mates glare at me. I can't believe I have done it again! After a while, Brett gets to his feet and walks over to me. He holds out his hand.

'Next time, just play the ball rather than the player, eh?'

I shake his hand then quickly walk away. I don't think I will ever manage to live that one down.

The last class of the day is a new one, Driver Education. There is a group of us who are nearly old enough to get our licences. I am in the class, and so are Henri, Linh and Brett. Tamiko is too young, so she rushes off to catch her train, trying hard to pretend she is happy to be finishing early rather than joining us. We all chat as we wait for the teacher to come in, looking forward to learning about cars and licences and trying to make out we have heard all about it before. Even Brett seems to have forgiven me for our earlier mishaps, as he sits in the centre of the group, talking about going to the pub on the weekend. Everyone crowds around him, enjoying his jokes and easy conversation.

The class starts, and we all sit back and talk about road rules and driving habits. We laugh as the teacher puts up an overhead of the best and worst drivers, and we talk for a while about the ridiculous things we have seen on the road. Someone has a story about a person driving with a dog on their knee, and there is another about a car with the petrol tank tied to its roof. Then the teacher pulls out a pile of papers and starts handing them out. There are murmurs around the room as she says that before we leave, we each have to read one road rule to the class and then explain it. We all start looking at each other – usually at TAFE we don't have to read aloud because there are so many of us who can't read and write.

A few people start shuffling their bags on the floor and looking at their watches. I slide a little closer to Linh in my chair, hoping that the teacher won't see me. Linh puts her hand up and offers to go first. She reads her rule easily and then shrugs her shoulders when she is asked to explain it. I stand my folder up on the desk and slide low in my seat so I can hide behind it. Someone else reads a rule, and there is more discussion about what it means. We slowly work our way around the class. There is one rule left on the page, and only me and Brett to go. I look at Brett and his face is red, staring at the paper in front of him.

'How about you, Brett?" the teacher asks. The class all look at him, and his face turns an even deeper shade of red. In an instant, I realise. Tall, gorgeous Brett – most popular kid at TAFE – can't read! The room is silent and the teacher smiles at him. He looks desperately around the room. Everyone is silent.

I take a deep breath and then start to read as clearly and loudly as I can.

'When driving towards an int … inter …' I pause, struggling over the words. Linh whispers to me 'intersection'.

'Intersection,' I continue. 'When approaching an intersection, it is important to obey the rel ... rel ...' I pause again.

'Relevant,' says the teacher.

'... relevant signs. These may be a stop sign, give-way sign or perhaps a roundabout,' I finish quickly.

'Is that enough?' I ask.

'Yes, well done Frances,' says the teacher. 'You've done a great job. That's enough for today everyone. We'll finish the rest next week.'

As the class hurries for the door, Brett walks over to me.

'Hey thanks for that – you really helped me out there.'

'No problem,' I say. 'It didn't look like you were any happier about reading than I was. Glad I could finally make it up to you!'

He smiles at me and it seems like we are finally equal somehow. He is no longer the impressive, exciting person I had once thought. Instead he is just Brett, who can play basketball like a dream but can't read a word. And I am not the frizzy-haired teenager trying too hard to impress, but just a girl who likes to help people out when she can. Perhaps the events of the past few days have taught us both something important.

Activity suggestions for beginning readers

These activities will be useful for students who have limited reading skills, and who will prefer to listen to the story rather than reading it independently. The activities cover a range of presentation types in order to cater for a variety of preferred student learning styles. The use of concrete objects can help students to retain information presented during these activities, and can be used as a way of teaching key words from the story.

1. **Lotions and potions** – Bring a number of hair and skin care items into class and spend some time discussing the use of each one with students. Items to try might include:

    - hair brush and comb
    - hair dryer
    - moisturiser
    - razor
    - shaving cream
    - after shave
    - nail polish
    - deodorant
    - sunscreen
    - mirror
    - eyeliner pencil

    Talk about why each item is used, which part of the body it should be used on, and the meaning of any warnings or hazards. Students may enjoy drawing a picture of a person and arranging the items around the picture with lines indicating where they should be applied or used.

2. **Clothing poster** – Make a poster using photographs cut from magazines or hand-drawn pictures that show examples of clothes which would be appropriate for various situations or which give particular unspoken messages. Examples might include:

    - clothes to wear to a job interview
    - clothes for an office-based job
    - clothes for an outdoor job
    - clothes to wear when going out for dinner
    - clothes for a casual party with friends

    Interesting discussions can result from introducing the subject of provocative clothing, and you may find there are some unexpectedly firm opinions about what is acceptable and what is not. Be aware that students from some cultural or religious backgrounds may find a discussion on provocative clothing to be offensive. Modify the activity if this is the case.

3. **Price check** – Visit a shopping centre and check the prices of a few 'wardrobe essentials' such as jeans, straight black skirt, shirt with a collar, or a pair of sneakers. Compare the price of similar items in a number of shops and record the information in a way which suits the writing skills of your students. This activity can be modified or extended by using some of the following ideas:

- Finding examples of various types of clothing in a department store (jeans, jumpers, skirts, jackets, socks, sneakers, underwear)
- Finding particular sections in a department store (women's clothing, baby wear, music, sporting goods)
- Finding prices for all the clothes needed for a job interview
- Finding prices for all the clothes needed to go out to a party
- Graphing price information for particular pieces of clothing
- Calculating how the price of an item will change when it is reduced by 20% during a sale

4. **Size, colour and style** – Visit a shopping centre and show students how to check the sizing and fit of various clothing items, and how to locate and use the fitting rooms in a shop. Also discuss how to choose colours and styles which are suited for particular purposes. Find examples of clothes which go well together and some which do not. It can be useful to teach students strategies such as having one part of an outfit black or white, and then adding a brighter colour to it. It may be possible to find a retailer who is happy to talk to students about clothes selection, and to show them around their shop.

5. **Act it out** – Ask a group of students to choose a scene they remember from the story and act it out. Help them to choose roles such as director, actor, narrator, and props designer. Alternatively, students might feel confident using the theme of 'disastrous first meetings' to script and perform a short scene of their own.

6. **Word-storm game** – This activity is a variation on brainstorming. Tell students they have two minutes to think of as many words as possible which have something to do with 'people'. If students have an understanding of the various parts of speech, you could try asking them to think of adjectives which could be used to describe people. Otherwise, provide some suggestions to start them off, such as 'body parts', 'shapes and sizes', 'personalities' and 'actions'. Be prepared to introduce new prompts if the ideas start to fail. This activity works best with the teacher as scribe, so the students are free to concentrate solely on generating words rather than getting caught up on spelling or handwriting.

7. **Word-storm activities** – The words that were generated in the word-storm game can be used for a number of purposes. Try using them to make nonsense sentences, as part of a word bank for a game of hangman, as prompts for writing a paragraph describing someone they have imagined, or as a resource list for jazzing up a piece of writing.

8. **Body parts match up** – For this activity, the teacher needs to have prepared a list of adjectives that relate to people. Read an adjective out loud and ask students to match it with a part of the body. Encourage humour for this activity; not all the word pairs have to make sense! You may, however, need to remind students about appropriate language if you do not wish to have every part of the body described in vibrant detail. Examples might include:

- Fuzzy – nostril hair
- Stinky – feet
- Dirty – toenails
- Round – face
- Long – nose

An alternative to this activity is to make two sets of cards out of contrasting coloured cardboard. One set contains the names of body parts and the other has a range of suitable adjectives. Students take turns to flip over two cards to make their own word pairs.

9. **Attractions between people** – Have a discussion with students about the things that attract one person to another, and the things that might be considered a turn-off. Ask students to imagine they are just meeting someone for the first time. Have them draw a picture of that person, and then label all the things they can think of that are turn-offs in one colour pen and all the things which might make that person attractive in another colour.

Examples might include:

- **Attractive** – long hair, cute smile, bright eyes, kind, friendly, funny
- **Turn-offs** – bad breath, rude, straggly hair, talks too much, looks scary

An extension of this activity is to talk about how many of the things on their picture are physical, and how many are to do with personality or other features. Discuss which is the most important, and which they notice the most about their own friends. Also discuss strategies for managing physical turn-offs such as bad breath and straggly hair, and how to deal with people who are rude, scary or like to bully others.

What does it mean?

Use your dictionary or write your own meanings for each of these words.

1. Mission _____

2. Admiring _____

3. Impression _____

4. Clumsy _____

5. Casual _____

6. Charity _____

7. Gorgeous _____

8. Capable _____

9. Novice _____

10. Attractive _____

11. Competent _____

12. Collapse _____

Word opposites

Can you think of a word that is the opposite in meaning to each of the words below?

1. Most _____

2. Friend _____

3. Wavy _____

4. Forget _____

5. Gently _____

6. New _____

7. Sooner _____

8. Clever _____

9. High _____

10. Even _____

11. Stand _____

12. Forward _____

13. Join _____

14. Easy _____

Word endings

Draw a line to match each of these word endings with their correct beginnings. Next, choose five words and use them all in the same sentence. Be creative! Try writing out any unfamiliar words then seeing if you can spell them correctly on your own.

Six	nion
Trou	ience
Coun	ers
Opi	thing
Hor	try
Impress	teen
Any	able
Clum	ble
Exper	ions
Comfort	sy
Teach	ror

_____

_____

_____

_____

Choose the correct word

Circle the word that makes the most sense in each of these sentences. You may find that it helps if you or someone else reads the sentence aloud to see which option sounds better. Re-read the sentences out loud when you have finished.

1. Frances and Linh **(gone / went)** to school together.

2. Frances wore a **(pear / pair)** of high heels to TAFE.

3. There was chewing gum **(stick / stuck)** to the seat on the bus.

4. **(Their / There)** is no such thing as a last chance to make an impression.

5. The class were planning **(four / for)** the barbecue.

6. If you look in the **(draw / drawer)** you will find a hairdryer.

7. **(Except / Accept)** for Linh, Tamiko and Frances, very few people talk to Henri.

8. Frances would like to **(get / got)** Brett to notice her.

9. She **(new / knew)** she would have to try hard to get his attention.

10. It is important not to try **(to / too)** hard to make an impression.

11. Take a deep **(breathe / breath)** before you start to read.

12. You need a driver's **(licence / lisense)** before you can drive on the road.

Past tense

Past tense is a way of writing a word to show that something has already happened. Often we add a '**d**' or an '**ed**' to the word to make it into its past tense, but sometimes we have to learn a whole new word.

For each of the sentences below, write the word in brackets in its past tense form.

> **Hint:** Try putting a 'past' word such as 'Yesterday' at the start of the sentence.

1. Brett **(is)** _____ sixteen years old.

2. Linh and Frances **(go)** _____ to school together.

3. Frances **(has)** _____ mascara on her eyelashes.

4. She also **(wear)** _____ a long black skirt.

5. He **(choose)** _____ a new suit for his job interview.

6. Frances **(know)** _____ she had to make a good impression.

7. Brett **(think)** _____ everyone would laugh at him if he let them see he couldn't read.

8. Frances **(find)** _____ that Brett liked her more when she was herself.

9. She **(spend)** _____ a lot of time getting ready in the morning.

10. The teacher **(ask)** _____ Brett to read out loud.

11. Frances **(try)** _____ to think of something smart to say to Brett.

Sounds like ...

Rhyming words end with the same sound when you say them out loud. Lots of songs and poems contain rhyming words.

For each of the words below, see if you can think of three other words that rhyme with it.

The rain in Spain

Example: **Drain, main, plane, sane, explain.**

1. Read   _____   _____   _____

2. Spend   _____   _____   _____

3. Your   _____   _____   _____

4. Way   _____   _____   _____

5. Blink   _____   _____   _____

6. Time   _____   _____   _____

7. Ball   _____   _____   _____

8. That   _____   _____   _____

9. Look   _____   _____   _____

10. Bread   _____   _____   _____

11. Tall   _____   _____   _____

12. New   _____   _____   _____

Alphabetical order

A ... Z

These sets of words are from the story **First Impressions**. Put each set into alphabetical order, then see if you can write a sentence that contains all the words from one set.

1. actually, eyes, funny, decided, came, Henri

_____

_____

2. speak, listen, tell, call, whisper, explain

_____

_____

3. time, thought, forgotten, friends, bus, bothered

_____

_____

4. cheeks, eyes, head, eyelashes, teeth, nose

_____

_____

5. smell, strange, serious, shower, sister, she

_____

_____

6. last, lurk, Linh, look, like, lot, least, learn

_____

_____

7. road, rule, read, run, reach, right, roundabout, relevant

_____

_____

What's that short for?

A **contraction** is a way of shortening a word using an apostrophe. For each of the contractions below, write out the full words by adding in the letters that have been replaced with the apostrophe.

1. You've _____

2. Didn't _____

3. Can't _____

4. That's _____

5. Don't _____

6. Couldn't _____

7. We've _____

8. Doesn't _____

9. I'm _____

Now try rewriting these words and phrases using an apostrophe to shorten them and make your own new words. Remember that the apostrophe usually goes where the letter or letters have been left out of the word.

10. There is _____

11. We will _____

12. Had not _____

13. She is _____

14. Has not _____

15. He has _____

16. Have not _____

17. Was not _____

True or false?

Use this TRUE / FALSE quiz to check how well you read the story **First Impressions**. You may need to look back at the story for some of your answers.

1. Brett is sixteen years old.

    TRUE   FALSE

2. Frances is friends with Emily.

    TRUE   FALSE

3. Henri came to TAFE from a school in the country.

    TRUE   FALSE

4. Frances catches the bus to TAFE.

    TRUE   FALSE

5. Ivan is the teacher for the barbecue activity.

    TRUE   FALSE

6. Tamiko helps with the sauce and mustard at the barbecue.

    TRUE   FALSE

7. Frances throws the ball to Henri during the basketball game.

    TRUE   FALSE

8. Brett shoots a three-pointer during the basketball game.

    TRUE   FALSE

9. Linh is too young to join the Driver Education class.

    TRUE   FALSE

10. Brett is good at reading.

    TRUE   FALSE

Who did what?

For this activity, you need to reread the story **First Impressions** and find out which character did each of the things listed below. You may find it helps to read through all the questions first, then use a highlighter to mark answers that you find as you are reading.

1. Who went to school with Frances before they started TAFE?

    _____

2. Who is sixteen years old?

    _____

3. Who has a stutter?

    _____

4. Who is Frances trying to impress?

    _____

5. Who is the teacher for the barbecue class?

    _____

6. Who owns the black skirt?

    _____

7. Who helps Frances organise the barbecue?

    _____

8. Who has trouble reading out loud in class?

    _____

How well did you read?

Choose the correct word or phrase in brackets to complete each of these sentences about the story **First Impressions**.

1. The barbecue was organised as a _____
    [celebration for the end of term / fundraising activity / way of introducing new
    students to the TAFE].

2. Frances poured _____ [tomato sauce / mustard /
    soft drink] all over Brett's hand.

3. The last class of the day was _____ [Maths / English /
    Driver Education].

4. Frances had _____ [dirt / red texta / chewing gum] on her
    skirt from the bus seat.

5. When Frances fell over in front of Brett, the _____ [two / three /
    four] girls with him started to laugh.

6. Tamiko often gets in trouble because she _____
    [throws pens in class / teases other people / says the wrong thing].

7. Frances powdered her cheeks with _____ [pink / red / orange]
    blusher.

8. Francis woke up at _____ [7 am / 8 am / 6.30 am] so she could get
    ready to go to TAFE.

9. At Henri's old school in the country, other students _____
    _____ [called him names / poured glue into his pencil case /
    pushed him over].

10. Brett has _____ [blue / green / hazel] eyes.

11. Frances had _____ [coffee / Milo / tea] with her breakfast.

12. The class sells _____ [sausages / hamburgers / steaks]
    at the barbecue.

13. At the end of the first half of the basketball game, some of the students
    _____ [keep playing during the break /
    have a cigarette / go home].

Sentence endings

Can you write an ending for each of these sentences about the story **First Impressions**?

1. Tamiko and Frances ...

2. At the barbecue ...

3. Brett is ...

4. When Frances was on the bus ...

5. The class is good at ...

6. Henri, Linh and Tamiko ...

7. Frances felt embarrassed when ...

8. Most people at the TAFE ...

9. Frances realises that ...

10. Frances learns to ...

11. To make a good impression ...

12. Ivan would like his class to ...

Your own first impression

When people first meet you, what would their overall impression be? Would they see you as someone who was confident, shy, sporty, artistic, friendly, or maybe a combination of lots of things? Use this chart to record some of the things other people might notice about you, as well as some things you think about yourself.

As a friend

Physical characteristics

Your name

_____

Best assets

Personality

Impressions of a friend

For this activity, choose a friend and write a few comments in each box to say what impresses you most about them. Use positive comments only – remember, you are writing about what **impresses** you about them.

Great things they have done	Physical appearance

Your friend's name

_____

Personality	Their goals for the future

Character profiles

A character profile tells us some of the most important details about a character from a story. Write or draw a character profile for each of the people listed below. Include all the details you can from the story, then add some ideas of your own.

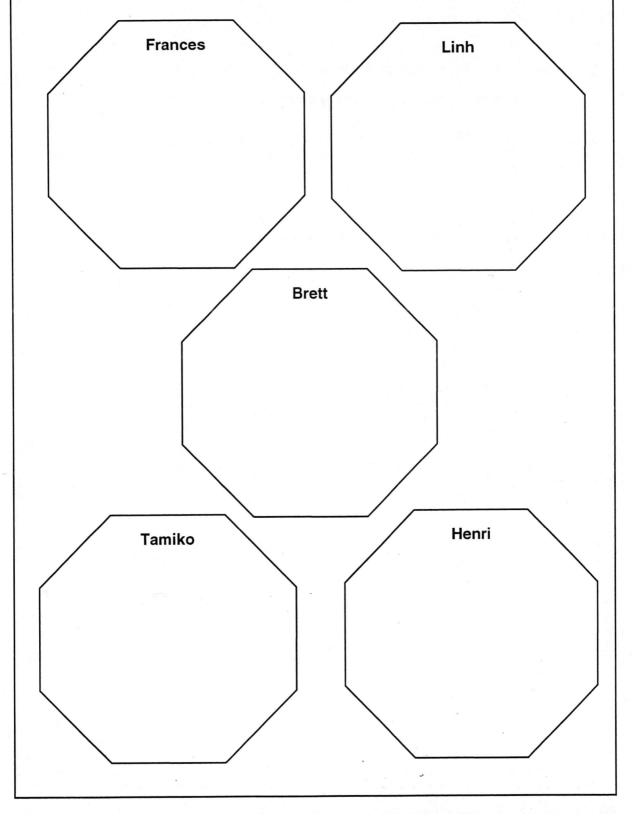

Frances

Linh

Brett

Tamiko

Henri

What impresses you?

When you are checking someone out as a potential new boyfriend or girlfriend, what do you look for? Are you impressed by new clothes and a gorgeous body? Someone who can make you laugh? Someone with similar interests to your own? Someone who likes to party all night and sleep all day? Someone who studies hard and knows what they want to get out of life?

Write a paragraph describing what impresses you. Use some of these sentence starters to help give your paragraph some shape, or just write your own.

My ideal boyfriend / girlfriend would be …

He / she would have …

He / she would like to …

He / she would always …

When I wanted to talk, he / she would …

Together we would …

He / she would make me feel …

He / she would own …

He / she would look like …

Writing skills for work

For most jobs you need to be able write at least at a basic level to do your job properly. Even in jobs which involve mostly practical tasks, you will probably still need to do things such as fill out forms or take orders or phone messages. Choose **3** career areas and think of at least **5** examples of the types of writing you would need to do.

***Example:* Career area – Hairdressing**

Writing skills needed:

1.   client bookings taken over the phone

2.   orders for supplies

3.   pricelists on advertising boards

4.   reference for a work experience student in your shop

5.   forms for paying superannuation for an employee

Career area _____

Writing skills needed:

_____

_____

_____

_____

_____

_____

_____

_____

_____

_____

_____

_____

_____

_____

continued ...

Career area _____

Writing skills needed:

_____

_____

_____

_____

_____

_____

_____

_____

_____

_____

_____

_____

_____

_____

Career area _____

Writing skills needed:

_____

_____

_____

_____

_____

_____

_____

_____

_____

_____

_____

_____

_____

_____

Where are you headed?

Sometimes it is good to stop and think about what you want to get out of life and where you are headed. Are things going along OK, or are you looking for a change? Do you need to think about life after school, or maybe start planning the subjects you will choose later on? Fill the chart in below with some ideas about yourself in a few years time.

Jobs I might like to try

Places I might like to live

Hobbies or activities I might like to try

The sort of family I would like to be a part of

Looking the part

When you are trying to make a good impression, the clothes you choose and your overall presentation are important.

Work with a partner to draw two potential job seekers. Both of them are applying to work as a trainee office receptionist for a small business in the city. One job seeker is definitely not suitable; the other is the perfect candidate.

Draw each job seeker and label all the items which made the difference!

Successful job seeker

Unsuccessful job seeker

Planning what to say

Sometimes you need to be able to think of the right words to say, fast! In **First Impressions**, Frances had trouble thinking of things to say that would impress Brett. She forgot to plan what she wanted to say, and the conversation failed.

For each of the situations below, work with a partner to think of **3** sentences to use during the conversation.

Ummmm ...

Situation one:

You have arrived for a job interview and you know you are about ten minutes early. You walk up to the counter and the woman sitting there says, 'Yes, can I help you?'

Situation two:

You would like to start a conversation with the good-looking girl who is in the same art class as you. You have been introduced to her before, but you cannot remember her name.

Situation three:

You want to negotiate with your teacher to get an extension for an English assignment that you have not yet finished.

Situation four:

You are trying to think of a really good reason to give your parents for being an hour late home from a party.

Situation five:

It is your turn to introduce yourself to a room full of people in a new class. You stand up in front of the group and say ...

Situation six:

You have phoned in response to an advertisement in the paper for a jeans shop that would like to employ a junior sales assistant to work on weekends. When you are put on to the right person, the voice on the phone says, 'This is Lisa Jefferson. You've phoned about the job?'

Interviewing people

Find three people who are happy to be interviewed on the topic **Who impresses you?** Use the questions below as a guide, but add some more of your own. Collect all your answers and put them together in a way that you find easy to read. Present a summary of your findings to a small group of students. You may find this easier to do if you write out some prompts for your talk.

Your name _____

Name of person being interviewed _____

Date of interview _____

Who is the person who most impresses you most in life? (It can be someone you know or someone you have never met.)

_____

Can you tell me a bit about that person?

_____

_____

_____

What is it about him or her that impresses you?

_____

_____

Have you ever met this person / would you like to meet this person one day?

_____

_____

Extra questions / answers:

_____

_____

_____

_____

_____

It pays to have a reply

It is as important to be able to answer questions as it is to ask them in a conversation, and it takes practice!

Try writing out some responses to these common conversation questions. Make your answers as interesting as possible, and avoid using single word answers.

? Do you live close to here?

_____

_____

? Do you have a large family?

_____

_____

? What sort of music do you like?

_____

_____

? What do you think of this subject?

_____

_____

? What did you do on the weekend?

_____

_____

? Do you play a sport?

_____

_____

? Do you go to work?

_____

_____

? What are you going to do on the holidays?

_____

_____

Starting conversations

Starting a conversation with someone new can be a challenge, and often you can feel a bit awkward and lost for words. Remember that the other person may be feeling just as awkward as you! If you plan your sentences in your head first, it can help the words to flow a bit more easily.

Think of a sentence or two on each of these topics that you could use to start a conversation.

A way of introducing yourself

_____

_____

A way of introducing a friend to a group of people

_____

_____

Finding out the time

_____

_____

Borrowing something from another person

_____

_____

Getting directions to a room in an unfamiliar building

_____

_____

A recent football game

_____

_____

The weather

_____

_____

A program that was on TV

_____

_____

General knowledge topics

Knowing a bit about your own city, state and country is useful when you are talking to other people. Test your general knowledge of Australia with this quick quiz.

1. What is the name of the country in which we live?

2. What is the name of the state or territory in which we live?

3. What is the name of our capital city?

4. What is the name of our suburb (or town)?

5. What is the name of our national anthem?

6. Can you name one other state?

7. What is the capital city of Australia?

8. Do you know the name of one sport that is popular in our state?

9. Can you name one team who plays that sport?

10. Can you name the captain of that team?

11. Who is the prime minister of Australia?

12. How old do you have to be to vote in Australia?

13. Name one Australian band and the name of one of their songs or albums.

14. Can you name a major river in our state (or territory)?

15. Can you name a politician other than the prime minister?

16. Do you know the name of another country which is close to Australia?

17. What is Uluru also known as?

18. Can you name the leader of another country?

19. Describe the Australian flag.

20. What famous Australian song has the initials W_____ M_____?

What really matters?

Often we are impressed by different aspects of the people we meet. Sometimes we are impressed by appearance, at other times we are more impressed by good work skills and an ability to get a job done on time. Work with a partner to decide what sort of **personality, skills, knowledge or characteristics** would be important for each of these situations.

A factory worker doing the same tasks every day	**A babysitter looking after a crying toddler**
A teenager who wants to start their own band	**An athlete who wants to be selected for a national team**
A student who is being told they are about to fail all their subjects at school	**A work experience student on their first day at a vet surgery**

What sort of impression should you make?

For each of the situations below, think about the sort of impression you would try to give. What would you wear, how would you act, and what would you say? Your research for this activity might involve talking to other people, or looking on the internet to find tips on presentation for job interviews.

Going on a first date

Clothes	Hygiene / personal care
Speaking and listening	Body language

Going for a job interview

Clothes	Hygiene / personal care
Speaking and listening	Body language

Surf the net and look into TAFE

TAFE offers many interesting courses you can study once you leave school. Some have special entry requirements, such as a Year 10 pass. For others, you may need to buy certain equipment or clothing.

Choose **3** of the career areas below. Use the internet to research the following information about each of the areas you have chosen :

1. The name of a course and a TAFE at which it is offered.

2. The entry requirements for the course.

3. Any costs or equipment you would need.

4. The length of the course.

5. A job you could get once you finished the course.

- ▢ Hospitality

- ▢ Automotive

- ▢ Foreign language

- ▢ Sport and recreation

- ▢ Writing

- ▢ Bartending

- ▢ Office skills

- ▢ Animal husbandry

- ▢ Desktop publishing

Look into exercise

Exercise is an important part of staying fit and healthy, but it is sometimes hard to fit into a busy lifestyle. Frances in **First Impressions** enjoys being fit and active, and likes playing games such as basketball with her classmates.

Use your research skills to look into the questions below. You can organise your work in any way you choose, but it must be clearly set out and easy to read.

Find five (5) benefits from doing regular exercise.

_____

_____

_____

_____

Find five (5) risks from not doing any regular exercise.

_____

_____

_____

_____

_____

How much exercise should we do?

_____

_____

_____

Is there such a thing as doing too much exercise? Why / why not?

_____

_____

Why do some people give up exercising as they get older?

_____

_____

_____

Aerobic effort

Aerobic effort means how hard our heart and lungs are working during exercise. Some activities take a lot of aerobic effort, such as the basketball game Frances plays in **First Impressions**. Other activities can be done so that our heart and lungs are not working as hard.

Organise the activities below into columns according to whether they are a high, medium or low aerobic effort.

High intensity	Medium intensity	Low intensity

sleeping	swimming freestyle laps	paddling in the pool
reading	sitting	ten-pin bowling
sprinting	riding up a steep hill	brisk walk
playing a round of golf	hard game of basketball	cheering at the footy
kicking the footy	playing a footy game	5 km flat bushwalk
sitting in a row boat	kick-boxing class	white-water rafting
10 km steep bushwalk	canoeing in flat water	gentle bike ride
sailing the Sydney to Hobart	shooting a few baskets	
sailing in windy weather		

| Unit 2 First Impressions: Learning checklist | Name: | | |

This checklist allows you to keep track of the worksheets and activities that you have agreed to complete with the help and support of your teacher. Once you have agreed on the activities you are going to do for this unit, you can use the checklist as a tool for remembering what you need to do and for keeping a record of your achievements.

Worksheet / activity	Tick if chosen	Date completed	Checked by
2.2 What does it mean?			
2.3 Word opposites			
2.4 Word endings			
2.5 Choose the correct word			
2.6 Past tense			
2.7 Sounds like ...			
2.8 Alphabetical order			
2.9 What's that short for?			
2.10 True of false?			
2.11 Who did what?			
2.12 How well did you read?			
2.13 Sentence endings			
2.14 Your own first impression			
2.15 Impressions of a friend			
2.16 Character profiles			
2.17 What impresses your?			
2.18 Writing skills for work			
2.19 Where are you headed?			
2.20 Looking the part			
2.21 Planning what to say			
2.22 Interviewing people			
2.23 It pays to have a reply			
2.24 Starting conversations			
2.25 General knowledge topics			
2.26 What really matters?			
2.27 What sort of impression should you give?			
2.28 Surf the net and look into TAFE			
2.29 Look into exercise			
2.30 Aerobic effort			

Unit 3: Out of Work

Before reading the story

Pre-reading activities are useful for all students before beginning a new unit of work. Activities such as these will help teachers establish the level of student understanding of basic concepts contained within the story, and give students a framework for topics to be covered during the unit.

1. Check if students understand the term 'self-esteem'. Discuss self-esteem, particularly in relation to job-seeking. Talk about strategies for keeping your self-esteem high while looking for work.

2. Ask students if they have ever looked for work before, and discuss any jobs currently done by students in the group.

3. Talk about languages other than English which are spoken by students in the group, and discuss how the ability to speak another language can be an asset when applying for jobs.

4. Make a list of job categories on a whiteboard or large sheet of paper, then ask students to list various jobs under the headings provided. Headings to use might include:

    *   outdoor jobs
    *   technical / computing jobs
    *   jobs involving people
    *   office jobs
    *   hospitality jobs
    *   medical jobs

5. Check that students are familiar with the following words and phrases:

    *   resume
    *   job application
    *   interview
    *   employer / employee
    *   training
    *   career counsellor
    *   job interests survey
    *   advertisement
    *   dole
    *   motivation

6. Make a flowchart of the job-application process based on current student understanding. How do they imagine they might go about getting a job? This chart can be revisited later in the unit and modified as needed.

About the story

Looking for work can be difficult. Finding work can be even more so. Sometimes when a person has been trying for a long time to find work they can end up feeling pretty down and miserable. They might even feel like giving up the search for work altogether. After all, being on the dole isn't so bad, is it?

But sometimes, you can have someone on your side who makes a difference to how things turn out. Someone who believes you can do it. Who knows you are going to succeed. Who is determined that you will not give up until things turn out the way you want them to.

In **Out of Work**, you will meet Toula, who has been trying for months to find a job. Toula has a lot to offer a potential employer. There is her cheeky attitude, her quick temper, her unusual dress sense and her ability to always put her foot in it. You will also meet Ellen, Toula's long-suffering career counselor. It is Ellen's job to try to find Toula work. Ellen loves a good challenge, and she certainly finds one when she agrees to work with Toula!

Read **Out of Work** and see how things turn out for Toula during her search for work.

- Does she eventually manage to stop saying the wrong thing to the wrong person?

- Does she learn to get places on time?

- Does she become a waitress, animal shelter assistant or charity collector?

- Does Ellen succeed at her challenge?

- Is Toula destined to stay out of work forever?

Out of Work

Toula knocks on the door of the careers office and waits, her long green nails tapping against her diary. She drops her cigarette on the ground and grinds it out with her shoe.

'Come in,' a voice calls.

'I'm in already Ellen,' she jokes as she closes the door behind her with a loud bang.

'Have a seat Toula,' says Ellen, as Toula plonks herself in the chair with a sigh and stretches her long legs out across the room.

'So. Found the ideal job for me yet Ellen? You know the one. Start at eleven, finish at one and an hour off for lunch?' asks Toula, looking hopefully in the direction of the coffee machine.

Ellen smiles. She is used to Toula's jokes. Ellen has worked with Toula for nearly four months now, and has become one of the more constant forces in her hectic young life. The weekly appointments are an event that Toula secretly looks forward to, although she would die rather than admit to Ellen that she actually enjoyed coming to see her.

Ellen has decided it is time to start encouraging Toula to make more of an effort to find work, although she is not sure how easy a task this will be. Ellen knows that Toula has fairly strong ideas about work. She doesn't like early starts (according to Toula, this means anything before ten-thirty). She doesn't want to do a job that doesn't pay well (it has to be double the dole to be worth the trouble, says Toula). And she refuses to change her appearance for anyone (Toula believes everyone should be allowed to wear green nail polish and a nose ring if they want to). But Ellen has some strong ideas of her own, and one of them is that Toula is not going to be her first failure as a career planner. She tries for a direct approach. She takes Toula's file from her desk and opens it.

'Toula. Let's look through your job interests survey from last week. We need you to start applying for some jobs that relate to your interest areas.'

'What's this "we" bit, Ellen? Anyway, don't you want to know what I've been doing this week? And is the kettle boiled? I'd kill for a cuppa.'

'No, Toula. I don't want to know about your week. And we're out of milk, so there's no coffee on offer. Now. Your survey.'

Toula rolls her eyeballs and takes the survey from Ellen.

'All right. If we must. But I'm telling you now, no one is going to employ me for anything reasonable. No one wants to pay me the right money, and it's too hard to get to anywhere because I don't have a car. And …'

'Stop,' says Ellen quietly. 'We're going to find you a job. It may not be the highest paying job in the world. It may not be exactly where you would like it, and it may not be your first choice of career, but we are going to find you one. And we are starting now.'

Toula looks at her in surprise. Ellen is normally a pushover for a coffee and a chat. What's going on?

'Ellen? Have the aliens taken you away and replaced you with someone else? Have they wiped coffee and polite conversation from your memory banks? It's me – Toula. The one that everyone says will never find a real job. Remember me?' Toula grins at her, but Ellen is not in a smiling mood.

'Yes Toula, I remember you. And we are going to find you a job, and you will do well at it.' Ellen reaches for the paper.

Toula shrieks in horror and dives onto the floor. 'No! Not the paper! Anything but the paper!'

'Get up Toula, you're acting like an idiot,' says Ellen.

Toula picks herself up from the floor and sits miserably in her chair again. 'I'm telling you now Ellen, there will be nothing in that paper that I can do.'

'Rubbish,' says Ellen looking through the pages on her desk. 'All we need is a job that doesn't start too early in the morning, doesn't involve much writing, pays well, doesn't need a Year 12 pass and is close to public transport. That shouldn't be too hard to find.'

Toula looks at her sideways. 'Have you been out in the sun too much over the weekend Ellen?'

'I'll do a deal with you, Toula,' she says. 'If I can find you a job that fits with all those things I just said, will you at least apply for it?'

'If you can find a job that fits with that list Ellen, I will not only apply for it, I will even go to the interview!' says Toula happily. 'Come on, wonder career planner, let's see what you can find!' Toula sits back in her chair, beaming happily at Ellen.

Ellen opens the newspaper to a page she had marked earlier in the day.

She points to an advertisement she has already circled in red pen.

Waiting Staff
Afternoon shift at busy Rundle Street cafe. Training provided, no experience needed. Above award wages plus tips.

'It's even close to the bus stop,' says Ellen.

'I'll give you a tip Ellen,' says Toula, frowning. 'I'll never get it.'

'Remember our deal Toula? "I will not only apply for it, I'll even go to the interview" were the words you used I think.'

Toula pales slightly, but true to her word, she reaches for the paper and reads through the advertisement.

'So you want me to like, phone them up and talk to them, don't you? You're not even going to set up an interview for me?'

'Nope,' says Ellen. 'You're on your own. Give it a go.'

She points to the phone on the desk.

'Why don't you give them a call now?'

Ellen stands up and walks across the room.

'While you're making your call, I'll get some milk then make us both a coffee.'

Ellen leaves the office to give Toula some privacy while she is on the phone. She knows that using phones and talking to strangers is something that Toula finds difficult, and she is not holding out too many hopes for success. But she also knows that Toula needs to get out into the job market and start trying for some jobs. She shudders as she hears Toula's raised voice from behind the door. There is a pause followed by Toula's voice again then a bang as the phone is slammed down hard. Ellen waits for a few minutes before walking back into the room. Toula is standing behind her desk, casually flicking through the pages of Ellen's diary. Her face is red and angry. Ellen walks quickly across and shuts the diary.

'Are you right there, reading my stuff?' she says crossly.

'Yeah, fine thanks. You spelt my name right for a change. And what do you mean by "needs motivation"? I'm motivated. You just don't like my style of motivation. It's the quiet, relaxed style. I'm getting ready mentally for the next big event in my life. In this case, lunch! Oh yeah, and the job sucked.'

'Uhuh,' says Ellen quietly. 'Want to tell me what happened? It didn't sound like you hit it off too well with your potential new boss.'

'Pig's bum he's going to be my boss. I wouldn't work for him in a fit. Sexist pig! He told me I'd have to do training! Like I'm going to go running and work out and stuff just so I can do his stupid job! I bet he wanted me to do training just so he could see me in a T-shirt and bike shorts! What a pervert! What does training have to do with working in a cafe anyway?'

Ellen sighs and looks at Toula.

'Training,' she says patiently, 'means learning about your job before they employ you. They would probably train you in serving customers, using the till, and making coffee. He didn't mean he wanted you to go running.'

'Oh,' says Toula. 'So I probably shouldn't have told him to stick his training up his …'

'No!' interrupts Ellen. 'You most definitely should NOT have told him to stick his training anywhere at all. Never mind, it's all learning I guess. Just maybe try not to yell at people quite so much Toula. Sometimes they are just trying to help you out.'

* * * * * * * *

The next week, Ellen tries a different approach. When Toula arrives, she hands her a single page with an address typed on it. Toula reads slowly from the page.

Norwood Animal Shelter

**277 Fullarton Road North
Norwood**

Ellen explains. 'The man who runs the shelter rang me yesterday. He's looking for someone to work part time with the cats and dogs at the shelter. They get a lot this time of year that people have dumped after Christmas. The shelter cares for them while they are trying to find them new homes. It wouldn't be an easy job though. They can't find homes for all the animals they get, so some of them have to be put down. You understand what that means, don't you? You wouldn't get too upset?'

'No, that's cool. I can cope with that. I've always liked animals, and it would be great to work outside rather than being stuck inside all day. Hey Ellen. There's no phone number here. How am I supposed to get in touch with them if you don't give me the phone number?'

Ellen looks at her and smiles. 'You really think after last week I'm going to let you ring the man and talk to him over the phone? We – you – have an interview at 2 pm. If we leave now, we should be just in time.'

The drive from Parkside to Norwood does not take long. As they drive past the racecourse, they stop briefly as a horse and rider cross the road in front of them.

'Hey Ellen!' says Toula excitedly. 'If this job doesn't work out, I could always be a jockey like that guy! I reckon I could be good at that!'

Ellen glances across at where Toula is sitting with her knees wedged up against the dashboard, her head nearly touching the roof.

'I hate to break this to you Toula, but there's not much call for 5 foot 9 inch jockeys. Your legs would be dragging along behind you down the track!'

'Hey,' says Toula. 'I thought you were supposed to be boosting my confidence, not cutting me down like a tree!'

'Just trying to be realistic,' says Ellen.

When they arrive at the shelter, Ellen says that she is going to stay in the car. She watches as Toula walks across the yard and knocks loudly on the office door. There is no answer, and Ellen sees Toula knock again then reach out and try the door handle. Before she can get out of the car to stop her, Toula has walked into the office, giving a loud "Yoohoo" as she enters. Ellen sighs. 'Oh no,' she mutters to herself. 'This is not going to be good.'

A few minutes later, Toula comes back to the car.

'Ageist,' she announces firmly to Ellen.

'Ageist?' asks Ellen. 'What exactly is ageist? And since when do we let ourselves into someone else's office calling out yoohoo as we go?'

'Just trying to be friendly,' says Toula. 'Anyway, they won't employ me because they're ageist. Isn't that what you call it when someone wants to give all the worst jobs to the youngest person? He made a real point of it. Youth wages he called it. And he wanted me to pick up poo all day! As if! How gross would that be?'

'I don't think he meant for you to pick it up with your bare hands. They have brooms and shovels for that. And wouldn't youth wages be better than no wages at all?'

'Ooh,' says Toula. 'I hadn't thought of it that way. Oh well. Let's go and see if that jockey bloke is still there. He was kind of cute. I can see me wearing silk and a fancy pair of riding boots to work, can't you?'

Ellen bites her lip and does not reply.

* * * * * * * *

The following week, Toula arrives late at the centre. When she finally knocks on Ellen's door, she is wearing board shorts and a crop top, with her hair dripping down her back. Ellen glares at her and points to her hair.

'What's this? Is the hairdryer broken at your place? Or is an 11.30 am appointment a bit early for you?'

Toula has never been good with sarcasm. She looks at Ellen in surprise and says, 'No, 11.30 is fine with me. I even had time for a swim at the pool before I came here. See – my hair is still a bit wet at the back I think.'

Ellen looks at the growing puddle of water on the floor. 'Yes, I had noticed that,' she says. 'Now that you're here, is there any chance we could get on with helping you find a job?'

'Oh you don't need to worry about that Ellen. I've found one myself for this week. Look!'

She holds out a bright pink flyer with a row of dollar signs across the top. The add reads:

$$$$$$$$$$$$$$$$$$$$$$$$$$$$$

Doorknock your way to a fortune and help others at the same time.

Work casually – you choose your hours.

Commission paid plus bonuses to top earners.

Ring now – limited places only.

'So have you rung them yet?' asks Ellen.

'No, the phone is out at our place, so I thought I'd use yours. That's okay, isn't it?'

'Go right ahead,' says Ellen. 'It's good to see you showing some initiative. But don't be surprised if this job is harder than you think.'

'Don't be negative, Ellen. I've read the add carefully, like you showed me. We both know I can knock on doors and talk to people, and I think I'd be good at the casual bit. You're always telling me I'm too casual, and now here is an employer that wants just that. Imagine if I'd stopped being casual just because you told me to!'

Ellen opens her mouth to speak then shuts it firmly again. She knows better than to try and stop Toula in mid flight. Toula is already on the phone, talking excitedly.

'Yes I've got a referee. Hang on, she's just here. I'll put her on.'

She passes the phone to Ellen. 'They want to talk to you about something,' she hisses. 'Don't blow this for me, will you?'

After a brief conversation, Ellen passes the phone back to Toula. Plans are made for Toula to pick up her charity tin from a city address that afternoon, followed by a two-day trial starting the following morning.

The next day, Ellen has a phone call. The man says he is Jack Collins, manager of collection services for a local charity. He is angry, and spends the next few minutes telling her about Toula's disastrous first morning as a charity collector. When he finally calms down, Ellen explains to him that Toula has a fairly quick temper, and that she is not yet used to the demands of the workforce. She asks him if there is any way that Toula could be given a second chance, but he tells her that Toula had set a new record at their charity. In just three hours, she had been the cause of seven complaints. Toula's days as a tin rattler were definitely over. Ellen hangs up the phone, makes herself a coffee and waits for Toula to arrive. Sure enough, a few minutes later her coffee break ends as Toula comes stomping through the door.

'Bloody racists! They should all be thrown out of the country! Just because I'm Greek, they don't want me at their stupid charity. And the people I had to doorknock were just as bad. Mean, just plain mean. Wouldn't part with any money, even when I told them it was for a good cause. It's a set-up.

I'll bet the other collectors set the whole thing up just so I didn't get a chance to make any money.'

Toula pauses for breath, and looks at Ellen's face to see how much of her story she is buying.

'Toula. I don't think that people not giving money to a charity is really grounds for a conspiracy theory. And people like to have a choice about which charities they give money to. They don't have to give money to you just because you arrive on their doorstep. Anyway, how did the people at the charity know you were Greek?'

Toula's face reddens. 'Oh. You talked to them then. I dunno about how the boss knew I was Greek, but I'm sure he's a racist. He said something about never having met anyone like me before, but I didn't get what he meant.'

'I think I can clear that one up for you,' says Ellen. 'The man I spoke to said you kept some poor old guy standing on his porch for half an hour while you tried to get him to give you money and then when he finally told you to go away you abused him in Greek. Unfortunately for you, the man actually was Greek, so he understood every word you said. Even the bit about his garden gnomes. What exactly did you tell him, anyway?'

Toula giggles. 'You don't really want to know.'

'Right,' says Ellen. 'Next week is over to you. I'm going on a training course, and before you ask, no that does not mean I'm having a week off to go running in the park. You have to find the next job yourself. I'll see you the week after to hear how you've gone.'

* * * * * * *

Three weeks pass, and Ellen still hasn't heard from Toula. She tries to call her at home, but there is only a recorded message telling her the phone has been cut off. All she can do is wait and hope that everything is alright. Then one night, just as she is about to lock the office, Toula turns up. She is wearing dark pants and a blue shirt with a small logo on the sleeve. On her feet is a pair of work boots with mud caked up around the edges. Her nails are unpainted and her nose ring has been taken out.

Toula is about to walk into the office when Ellen yells, 'Feet! Mud! Not on my floor you don't. Where have you been and why haven't you rung me? I haven't heard from you in weeks and then you turn up like nothing has happened and think you can just tramp mud all over my floor. What a cheek.'

'Ooh. Sorry Ellen. I keep forgetting people have this thing about mud on their carpets. In our place it's just a good way of hiding the rest of the stuff that's on the floor.'

She takes her boots off and then does a little spin around the room in her socks.

'So what do you think of my new uniform? The blue suits me, don't you think?'

'It's great. But what's the uniform?'

Toula leans forward so Ellen can read the logo on her shirt. 'Adelaide Botanical Gardens. Nice shirt. You're not going to tell me you've got a real job, are you?'

Toula grins at her.

'Sure do. I'm a trainee gardener. Horti something or other they call it. I like gardener better myself. At least I can spell that. Anyway, I saw all these people at the Botanical Gardens the other week, and so I went up and started chatting to one of them about what they were doing. He said they were trainees working on a big project in the gardens. So I told him I was really good at gardening, which isn't strictly true but I thought it sounded better than telling him I didn't know a weed from a pot plant. And he said to come back and see him because there were still a few more vacancies on the program. So I did, and he gave me a job. Just like that! Well almost just like that. He said you just have to fill out some forms to say that I am eligible to be a trainee and then I can work there for a year.'

Toula places a large pile of papers on Ellen's desk.

'Oh, and he said he needs them first thing tomorrow. It's a good thing I saw you before you went home for the night, isn't it? Anyway, I'm off to the pool to wash off some of this mud. Okay if I pick these up about eight tomorrow?'

Ellen groans. 'Eight! I'm going to be here half the night doing these Toula. You couldn't have given me a bit of warning, could you?'

'Don't be silly Ellen,' says Toula with a smile. 'Real workers stay until the job is done. Didn't they teach you anything at career planner school?'

Activity suggestions for beginning readers

These activities will be useful for students who have limited reading skills, and who will prefer to listen to the story rather than reading it independently. The activities cover a range of presentation types in order to cater for a variety of preferred student learning styles. The use of concrete objects can help students to retain information presented during these activities, and can be used as a way of teaching key words from the story.

1. **How-to-find-work cards** – Make cards with the steps for applying for a job written or drawn onto them. Ask students to tell you what each card is about and then put the cards into the correct order.

2. **Job-seeking essentials box** - Bring in a box of 'essential job-seeking props' and ask students to name each one and give a reason for it being important when looking for a job. Objects to include in the box are:
   - alarm clock or clock radio
   - hair brush
   - toothbrush
   - iron or an ironed shirt
   - soap
   - sample resume
   - card with a phone number on it
   - map or street directory

3. **Safety gear** – Bring in a variety of safety items and ask students to think of a work situation where each one might be needed. Examples include:
   - workboots - automotive or building areas to protect feet from injury
   - apron – hospitality areas to protect against food splatters / hot oil
   - hair net – food areas where hair may drop into food
   - hair elastic – industry areas where hair may get caught in machinery
   - goggles – building, welding or chemical areas where eyes may be damaged by flying debris, burns or chemicals
   - plastic gloves – food or chemical areas where hands may be burnt or food contaminated

4. **Pictures** - Draw group pictures of a job seeker who is destined for success and one who is destined for failure.

5. **Job interviews** - Role model a series of inappropriate behaviours during a job interview and ask students to identify each of the behaviours. Students tend to appreciate extreme examples, so try acting out the following:
   - The job seeker who arrives late, looking at their watch as they rush into the room and then discovers they have left their resume at home.
   - The job seeker who puts their feet on the table, takes out a packet of cigarettes and offers one to the interviewer.
   - The job seeker who fidgets with jewellery, watch and hair, then looks at their feet during questions and quietly mumbles responses.

- The job seeker who arrives with their hair unbrushed wearing a footy beanie and dirty shoes and asks the interviewer the time because they don't want to be late to catch their bus home.

6. **Job support agency visit** – Visit a job support agency for a tour of the facilities and a talk by a staff member. It may be useful to research which agencies cater for people with disabilities in your area.

7. **Library visit** – Visit a local library and see what resources are available for job seekers. The library may have computers, photocopiers and useful resources available to students.

8. **Skills** – Help students to make or draw a list of their skills. Include any skills nominated by students, rather than limiting the list to strictly job-based skills. Promote abilities such as speaking another language, playing a sport, knowing about art and craft activities or being able to look after a younger sibling as important and valuable skills.

9. **Personal qualities** – Help students to make or draw a list of their personal qualities. Students may enjoy creating cartoon pictures of qualities such as friendly, outgoing, cheerful, team player, inquisitive, eager to learn, interested, motivated, talkative, or helpful. Some words may need to be discussed to check that students understand their meanings.

10. **Name, address, phone number** – Check that all students are able to write and/or recognise their own name, address and phone number. Encourage them to practise copying this information out neatly in a variety of formats such as onto a card, onto plain paper without lines, onto paper with ruled lines and onto a form or questionnaire.

11. **Phone calls** – Practise making pretend phone calls to inquire about a job. Ask students to practise saying and spelling their own name and address out loud and discuss why they might need this when phoning for a job description.

12. **Volunteer work** – Discuss what volunteer work is and why it can be a useful activity for students who may be looking for work. Brainstorm a list of possible locations for volunteer work. This might include:

   - Babysitting for family or friends (with appropriate supervision)
   - Local library stacking shelves
   - Visiting an aged care facility
   - Sports centre
   - Neighbourhood house

What does it mean?

Use your dictionary or write your own definitions for each of these words from the story.

Career   _____

Survey   _____

Interview   _____

Employ   _____

Experience   _____

Training   _____

Advertisement _____

Privacy   _____

Diary   _____

Motivation   _____

Trainee   _____

Waiting staff _____

Eligible   _____

What do they do?

Use a dictionary or the job section in a newspaper to find out what each of these people does at work. Write a short description for each one.

Receptionist _____

_____

Horticulturist _____

_____

Book keeper _____

_____

Boiler maker _____

_____

Desktop publisher _____

_____

Call centre operator _____

_____

Labourer _____

_____

Cabinet maker _____

_____

Car detailer _____

_____

Upholsterer _____

_____

Childcare worker _____

_____

Storeperson _____

_____

What is missing?

Fill in the blanks in these words from the story **Out of Work**. Use the clues to help you.

A D _ _ _ T I S E _ _ _ _	Lots of these in the paper
B _ _	A type of public transport
_ A I T _ _ _ _	Waits on tables in a restaurant
N E W S _ _ _ _ _	Read this to find a job
_ _ O N E	Use this to ring about a job
_ _ O N E N _ _ _ E R	Need one so an employer can ring you back about a job
D _ A R _	Use this to write in appointments
I N T E R _ _ _ _	Chance to tell an employer about yourself
M O T I V _ _ _ O N	Get up and go, makes you really want to do something
_ _ _ R E S S	Where you live
T R _ _ N	Learn to do a job, also a type of transport
W _ _ E S	Paid these each week or fortnight
L _ _ E	Not early
A P P O _ _ _ M E N T	Time to be somewhere
M A N _ _ _ _	Boss
_ _ _ A T I V E	Not positive
_ _ _ _ _ N E E	A person doing training
C A R _ _ _	Your pathway through work

Words with two meanings

In **Out of Work**, Toula is confused by the word *training* because she doesn't know that it has two meanings.

Each of these words from the story can have two meanings. Choose six words and write sentences for them which make their meaning clear. You may need a dictionary to help you.

page	beam	close	change
tip	leaves	even	watch
point	let	call	ring
right	pass	cheek	will
mean	park	serve	fit
top	run	pool	trial
add	referee		

_____

_____

_____

_____

_____

_____

_____

_____

_____

_____

_____

_____

_____

_____

Same sound, different spelling

Words with the same sound but a different spelling and meaning are called **homonyms**. See if you can think of the homonyms for each of these words from the story. There is a clue in brackets to help you.

1. Wait   _____ (you lift these)

2. One   _____ (didn't lose)

3. Die   _____ (make it change colour)

4. Through   _____ (ball)

5. Need   _____ (bread)

6. Where   _____ (clothes)

7. Real   _____ (fishing equipment)

8. Know   _____ (not yes)

9. Sun   _____ (not a daughter)

10. Hear   _____ ('Come _____!')

11. See   _____ (water at the beach)

12. Would   _____ (trees)

13. Be   _____ (makes honey)

14. Horse   _____ (no voice)

15. Been   _____ (vegetable)

16. Pair   _____ (fruit)

17. Sure   _____ (at the beach)

18. So   _____ (needle and thread)

19. Whole   _____ (don't fall in one)

Words for work

Put each of the words from the list below with the correct job area.

chef	vegetables	grass	sweat	chop	brake
mow	weed	panel	tyre	knife	plate
bounce	eat	coach	road	gym	serve
prepare	lettuce	aerobics	bread	boil	bake
roast	umpire	bumper	ignition	polish	swim
steering	oil	fitness	salad	stretch	plant
trim	mulch	sprinkler	tennis	football	run
cricket	weights	seedling	windscreen	drive	detail

Horticulture / gardening	Hospitality / cooking

Automotive / cars	Recreation / sports

Job matching

Match each of these job titles with their correct description.

1.	Bar attendant	Cares for elderly people
2.	Aerobics instructor	Works with horses in a racing stable
3.	Camp worker	Repairs cars
4.	Potter	Washes dishes and glassware
5.	Kitchen hand	Supervises babies and young children
6.	Computer assembler	Cleans, repairs and decorates fingernails
7.	Computer operator	Translates one language into another
8.	Stablehand	Sells products or services over the phone
9.	Interpreter	Buys and sells property for others
10.	Childcare worker	Uses software programs on a computer
11.	Telemarketer	Makes, decorates and fires pottery
12.	Nail technician	Organises outdoor camping activities
13.	Motor mechanic	Serves drinks in a bar
14.	Aged-care worker	Teaches fitness classes in a gym
15.	Panel beater	Creates floral arrangements
16.	Real-estate agent	Arranges indoor colours, spaces and lighting
17.	Interior designer	Repairs car bodies and panels
18.	Florist	Puts computer hardware together

The right words for the right job

In many jobs, there are words that you will use a lot. Practise spelling the words for the jobs below, and then think of **ten** commonly used words for the next three jobs.

WAITER / WAITRESS

coffee	tea	sandwich	milkshake	milk
margarine	salad	salt	pepper	cheese

SALES ASSISTANT

register	customer	receipt	goods	warranty
faulty	size	reduced	sale	fitting room

OFFICE WORKER / RECEPTIONIST

GARDENER

CHILDCARE WORKER

True or false?

Circle **TRUE** or **FALSE** for each of these statements about Toula's story. You may need to go back and re-read some of the story to find your answers.

1.	Toula has done a job interests survey.	TRUE	FALSE
2.	Toula does not drink coffee.	TRUE	FALSE
3.	Toula wants a job that doesn't start too early.	TRUE	FALSE
4.	Toula refuses to ring up about the waitressing job.	TRUE	FALSE
5.	The waitressing job is in Flinders Street	TRUE	FALSE
6.	Ellen explains what training means.	TRUE	FALSE
7.	The animal shelter job is full time.	TRUE	FALSE
8.	The animal shelter is in Norwood Road.	TRUE	FALSE
9.	Toula rings up about the animal shelter job.	TRUE	FALSE
10.	Toula is very short.	TRUE	FALSE
11.	Youth wages apply to the animal shelter job.	TRUE	FALSE
12.	Toula is late for her 11.30 am appointment.	TRUE	FALSE
13.	Toula does well at doorknocking.	TRUE	FALSE
14.	Toula rings about the doorknocking job.	TRUE	FALSE
15.	Ellen is Toula's referee.	TRUE	FALSE
16.	Jeff Collins works for the charity.	TRUE	FALSE
17.	Toula gets a job in the botanical gardens.	TRUE	FALSE
18.	Ellen has to have Toula's papers ready by 9 am.	TRUE	FALSE

How well did you read?

Answer these questions about Toula's story to see how carefully you read. Some of the questions ask you to give your opinion rather than just find information in the story.

1. What job does Ellen do?

2. How long has Ellen known Toula?

3. Is Toula lazy?

4. Does Ellen enjoy working with Toula?

5. What does Toula think about getting a job?

6. What type of job would Toula like to find?

7. Why doesn't Ellen give Toula the phone number for the animal shelter job?

8. What does the advertisement tell us about the waitressing job?

9. Why has Ellen written 'needs motivation' in her diary?

10. What is the address for the animal shelter?

11. What time is Toula's interview at the shelter?

12. How does Toula find the job in the botanical gardens?

13. What does 'horticulture' mean?

14. Why doesn't Toula get the animal shelter job?

15. What does Toula tell Ellen happened when she went doorknocking?

16. How many complaints did Jack Collins have about Toula?

17. Apart from English, what language does Toula speak?

18. What does Toula wear when she is working in the botanical gardens?

How do you see it?

For each of the situations below, draw how you see the place or event in your head. Read through that part of the story again so you can put in as much detail as possible.

Toula arriving at Ellen's office	Toula and Ellen after the phone call to the cafe
Toula going doorknocking	Toula telling Ellen about her new gardening job

Job interest areas

Think of **4** examples of jobs that fit into each of these categories.

Outdoor jobs	Indoor jobs
Jobs involving people	Jobs where you make or build something
Jobs where you travel	Technology jobs

Job categories

Rule up a page into five sections using the categories below as headings. Arrange the jobs from the list into their correct categories. You may find that some jobs fit into more than one category.

CATEGORIES

1. Creative jobs

2. Outdoor Jobs

3. Indoor Jobs

4. Jobs using communication

5. Jobs where you sell something

6. Jobs where you make, build or fix something

JOBS

dancer	receptionist	call-centre worker
writer	personal trainer	pizza deliverer
hairdresser	school teacher	plumber
gardener	architect	waiter
actor	sales assistant	photographer
mechanic	chef	web page designer
office manager	painter	florist
dog trainer	pamphlet deliverer	door- to-door sales
childcare worker	real estate agent	

About me

When you are writing a resume or going to an interview, it is helpful to think about questions an employer might ask. Use this worksheet to list some of your skills, qualities and experiences. There is a list at the bottom of the page with some words that may help you.

Personal qualities (the type of person you are)

Skills (things you are good at)

Work experience / jobs

Words you might like to use

reliable	conscientious	punctual	practical
artistic	computer literate	team player	reading
creative	writing	measuring	cleaning
neat	hard working	responsible	communicating

Resumes – you've got to have one!

Resumes are essential if you are going to apply for a job. Here are some headings to help you write your own.

Personal details

- Name
- Date of birth / age
- Address
- Phone number – home and / or mobile

Education / qualifications

- Include your school name, years attended and year level completed.
- You may want to list some subjects you have passed also.
- Include any qualifications or training you have done, such as first-aid certificates or retail training.

Work history

- Work experience, part-time or holiday jobs
- Include the name of the employer and when you worked there.

Personal qualities

Keep this to a few short points such as being punctual, reliable or committed.

Awards and achievements

This could include things like being in the premiership team for softball or completing a Queen's Scout program.

Other interests

- Hobbies
- Sports
- Other activities

Referees

- Names
- Position / job title
- Company / organisation name
- Phone number

Job application letter 1

Read through the letter below. Toula has made a few spelling errors, and some of her sentences need to be written more clearly. You may even decide that some of the things she has written do not belong in a job application letter. Rewrite the letter using neat handwriting or typing.

Mrs Jill Wren
Traineeships Manager
Adelade Botanical Gardens
POB ox 1200
Adelaid

july 23 2003

Dear Jill,

Hi! I wood so much love to be a trainee in your programme. I have heard a lot about the program and it sounds grate. My name is Toula and I have finished my year ten at high school and I past almost everything accept for maths because that was boring. I have filled out all the forms you sent to me and I have put them in with this letter. I have put my report in from school to and I have put in my letters from my referee. Her name is Ellen. Can I have the letters and report back though because they are my only copies. You can ring me anytime. See my resume for my phone number and my address. My experience in gardening is that I have helped my grandfather in his market garden during the holidays and last term I did a project at school where we learnt about all the native plants and helped to plant them and water and mulch them. Now we go back each month to cheque how they are doing.

Yours sinceerley

Toula

Job application letter 2

Read through the letter below. Can you find all the mistakes Toula has made?
Correct the letter then copy it out again using neat handwriting or typing.
Remember to check your spelling.

The Boss
Norwoood Animal Shelta
270 Fularton Road North
Norwod

March 15th 2003

Dear Boss,

I am writeing to you about the job at youre shelta. My career advisor said you wear looking for someone to work their. I am good at being with animals and I like working with them a lot. I really want to get a job. I wood like to work at youre shelta. I have a dog and a cat at home and I look after them and take them for walks and feed them and cut there nails and take them to the vet. I have worked at the vet last holidays and it was grate fun. I take my next doors neighbours dog for a walk because she is too old and it is hard for her to walk too far. He is a kelpie and his name is Max.

Can you ring me please about the job. This is my phone number 6 515 4009.

See you

Toula

Writing using key words

Being able to write important information using only a few key words is an important work skill. Write each of these paragraphs out again, using only the key words. You may find it is easier to use dot points instead of whole sentences.

Animal shelter assistant

My shift today is from 7 am to 12.30 pm. My jobs for this shift are to sweep the cages, change the water in the dogs' bowls, bring in five bags of kitty litter from the shed and put the kitty litter into the cats' trays. If I have time left over at the end of my shift I can photocopy the fundraising notices for the dinner next month and put them into envelopes.

_____

_____

_____

_____

_____

_____

_____

Horticulture trainee

Today is Friday February the 14th. This morning I have to mow the grass and trim the edges at 16 Smith Street. When I go to 27A Fredrick Avenue I have to weed the front garden beds and water the pot plants. I have to remember not to water the daphne plant with the pink flowers too much like I did last week. I also have to remember to sweep the front and back paths and spread some mulch on the vegetable garden. In the afternoon I have to check the plant guards and top up the mulch in the park on Settlers Avenue.

_____

_____

_____

_____

_____

_____

_____

_____

continued ...

Waiter / waitress

The people at Table 3 said they wanted to order some drinks and something to eat. They wanted three chocolate milkshakes, two salad sandwiches made with wholemeal bread, and one serving of lasagne. The lasagne needs to be the vegetarian one because the lady with dark hair and pimples said she is a vegetarian. The salad sandwich for the man with a big nose needs to have mayonnaise and the salad sandwich for the woman with glasses needs to have margarine.

_____

_____

_____

_____

_____

_____

_____

_____

Doorknocking for charity

Shift report for Wednesday 3 June

Worker's name – Annelise James

I collected from lots of houses today, and most of the people I met were really nice. I went along Smith Road (both sides) turned left into Rosetta Place and collected from all the houses on both sides, then went all the way down Pine Avenue. I only collected from the houses on the left hand side because the hill was really steep and I was getting too hot. At the bottom of Pine Avenue I went right into Sells Street and collected from both sides and then finished up by doing the right hand side of Elliot Avenue. I counted all the money at the end of the shift and I had $132.40 exactly. My shift was from 2 pm to 5.30 pm. I think I need some more sunscreen because I have run out (I dropped the bottle out of my bag and it rolled down a drain).

_____

_____

_____

_____

_____

_____

_____

_____

Dangers at work

With a partner, think of four possible dangers for each of these work places, then write a plan for reducing the risks. Present your ideas to the group.

Waiter / waitress in a busy, crowded outdoor café in the city

Horticulture trainee working on a foreshore environmental program to remove thorny thistles from sand dunes

Animal shelter assistant working with stray dogs and cats

Charity worker doorknocking to raise money in an inner-city suburb in the late afternoon and early evening.

About that job

For the job advertisements below, work with a partner to write a script for your initial phone inquiry or visit. What might you want to know about each job? What would you tell the employer about yourself?

Dental Nurse

Busy city practice

Casual including some weekends

Experience preferred

Ring after 5 pm on 4717 8298

STOREPERSON

No experience necessary – full training provided

Pack orders and restock supplies

Part time hours

Phone for interview on 5213 4500

Machine Operators

Busy factory in south-eastern suburbs

Top rates paid for experienced workers

Immediate start

Apply in person to 21 Southern Hwy

between 8.00 and 8.45 am Monday

Dancer

No experience necessary

Must be over 18

Paid daily

Call now for audition

Ph.2307900400

How would you apply?

Imagine you are applying for these two jobs from the story. Write a script for a conversation for each job, then practise each call with a partner.

$$$$$$$$$$$$$$$$$$$$$$$$$$$$$$$

Doorknock your way to a fortune and help others at the same time.

Work casually – you choose your hours.

Commission paid plus bonuses to top earners.

Ring now – limited places only.

ABC: This is ABC Charity Collections. Can I help you?

You say:

ABC: I'll just put you through to Mr Vanden in our Recruitment Department. Please hold.

Mr Vanden: Hello, you're ringing about the collection position?

You say:

Mr Vanden: Are you happy to do a phone interview now?

You say:

Mr Vanden: Can you tell me a bit about yourself?

You say:

Mr Vanden: Have you done any collection work before?

You say:

Mr Vanden: Can you give me some referees that I can contact?

You say:

Mr Vanden: Do you have any questions about the job?

You say:

Mr Vanden: Can you give me a contact number so we can let you know?

You say:

continued ...

Waiting Staff
Afternoon shift at busy Rundle Street cafe. Training provided, no experience needed. Above award wages plus tips.

Mark: Coffee on Rundle. Mark speaking.

You say:

Mark: Let me tell you a bit about the job. We're looking for someone to work afternoons from Thursday to Sunday. The shift you would work would be about four hours, but it might be longer if we're busy. We need someone who can work well under pressure and is a fast learner. I'm happy to provide training for the right person. Does that sound like you?

You say:

Mark: Have you ever done any waiting work before?

You say:

Mark: What other sort of work have you done in the past?

You say:

Mark: Are you looking for an ongoing job or just something short term?

You say:

Mark: Are you happy to work on weekends and holidays?

You say:

Mark: Do you have a resume that you can send to us?

You say:

Mark: Is there anything you would like to know about the job?

You say:

Mark: I'll look forward to reading your resume. Thanks for calling us.

You say:

Job interests quiz

Do this quiz with a partner to start you both thinking about the types of work you might enjoy. When you have finished, brainstorm a list of jobs you both might be interested in trying.

1. Do you like working out doors?

2. Do you like making things with your hands?

3. Do you mind getting dirty?

4. Are you able to lift heavy objects?

5. Do you like being around people?

6. Are you good with animals?

7. Can you convince other people to do what you want?

8. Do you enjoy reading and writing?

9. Are you neat and tidy?

10. Are you good at organising yourself?

11. Are you good at organising other people?

12. Do you feel sick at the sight of blood?

13. Are you good with computers?

14. Do you get bored easily?

15. Do you like to travel?

16. Can you give people directions?

17. Are you creative?

18. Can you get up early in the mornings?

19. Can you stay up late at night?

20. Do you like talking to people on the phone?

What skills do you need?

Read through the job skills list with a partner, then match each skill with a job. Talk with your partner about any other skills you would need to do each job, and present your information to the group.

Good with animals	Able to talk to people
Can read a menu	Can use a lawn mower
Can write quickly	Communicates well
Recognises plant types	Can shovel dirt and mulch
Can follow a map	Likes working outdoors
Not scared of dogs	Able to lift and carry tools
Can walk long distances	Can carry trays of food and drinks
Can prune branches	Knows how to feed cats and dogs
Has a good memory for faces	Able to sweep and mop kennels
Honest	Can fill out a receipt book

Doorknocking for charity	**Waiter / waitress**

Horticultural trainee	**Animal shelter assistant**

How to fail a job interview

Imagine you are an employer. You don't know it yet, but the worst possible job candidate is about to walk through your door for an interview. With a partner, use the ideas below to create a person who is *never, ever* going to get a job until they make some big changes! Act out an interview between the employer and the job candidate.

Appearance

Body language

Work history

Behaviour

Speech

Resume

Common job interview questions

With a partner, plan how you would answer some of these common job interview questions. Keep your answers brief and to the point, and avoid using 'umms' and 'I dunnos'. Practise speaking your answers out loud, and ask your partner for some feedback.

- Could you tell us a bit about yourself?

- What sort of work have you done in the past?

- Why would you be someone we would like to employ?

- Are you confident with using a computer?

- Are you able to work as part of a team?

- Can you work without supervision?

- Can you tell us some of your strengths?

- What are some of your weaknesses?

- We have misplaced your resume. Do you have another copy with you?

- If you got this job, how long would you stay with us?

- Do you have some questions you would like to ask about the job?

- Do you have the names of two referees that we can contact?

What to do when you are not working

If you have finished school and are not working, you need to have things to do during the day so you don't get bored. Work with a partner to come up with a list of activities to do if you were not working.

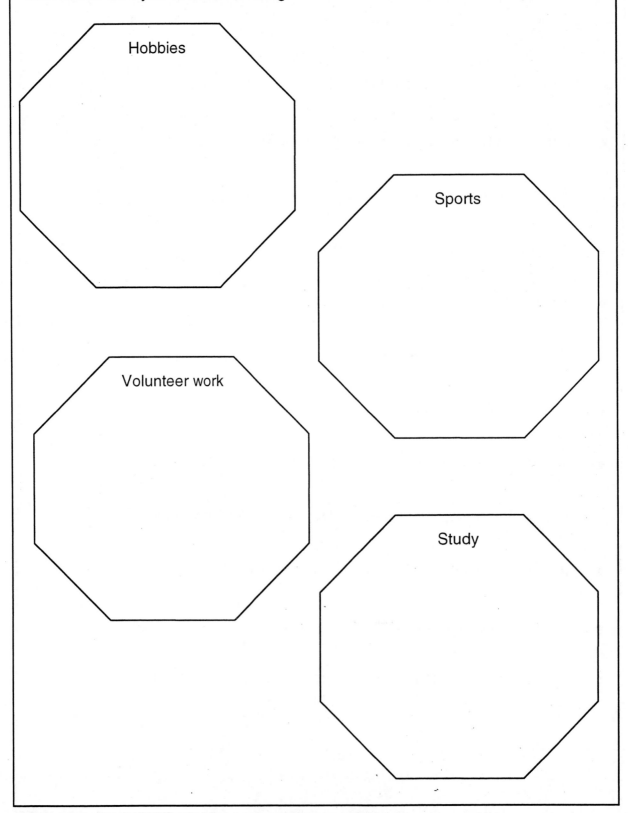

Make a map

If Toula went doorknocking for a job she would need to be able to read a map. Mapreading takes practice but it is easy once you get the hang of it.

Draw a map for each of the sets of directions below. Use a different coloured arrow to show the direction of travel.

Map 1

⇒ Travel along James Street, then turn right into Campbell Street.

⇒ Travel along Campbell Street to Gipps Street.

⇒ Turn left into Gipps Street, then left again into Regent Street.

⇒ Stop when you reach Princes Highway at the end of Regent Street.

Map 2

⇒ Start at the corner of South Terrace and Hutt Road.

⇒ Travel along Hutt Road then turn left into Wakefield Street.

⇒ Turn right at the corner of King William Street.

⇒ Turn left when you get to North Terrace.

⇒ Turn right into Montefiore Road and stop when you get to the Torrens River.

Map 3

⇒ Start at the jetty at Henley Beach.

⇒ Travel south along the Esplanade to Henley Beach Road.

⇒ Travel along Henley Beach Road to Tapleys Hill Road, then turn left.

⇒ Travel along Tapleys Hill Road to Grange Road, then turn left.

⇒ Travel along Grange Road to Frederick Road, then turn right.

⇒ Travel along Frederick Road to Jetty Street, then turn left.

⇒ Follow Jetty Street all the way to the jetty at Grange beach.

Map 4

⇒ Start at the roundabout at Jubilee Highway and Sutton Avenue.

⇒ Travel along Sutton Avenue to Gordon Street, then turn left.

⇒ Turn right into Lindsay Street, then left at Commercial Avenue.

⇒ Continue to the football oval at the corner of Victoria Street, then turn left.

⇒ Cross Jubilee Highway then turn left into Birdwood Avenue.

⇒ Turn right into Monash Crescent and finish your journey at the T-intersection of Montgomery Street.

Design a garden

Toula wants to learn about horticulture. One of the skills she will learn is how to design and lay out a garden.

Imagine you have been given this list of plants and other items to put into a garden. Create a design on a large piece of paper or cardboard to show how you have planned the garden.

- ❖ 5 tomato plants
- ❖ carrot seedlings
- ❖ lettuce seedlings
- ❖ broccoli seedlings
- ❖ 4 large trees
- ❖ 10 shrubs that need shade
- ❖ 10 shrubs that need full sun
- ❖ a display of small plants that will flower in spring
- ❖ 20 metres of garden edging
- ❖ 1 fish pond
- ❖ 1 cubby house
- ❖ 1 BBQ
- ❖ 1 rainwater tank
- ❖ 1 set of outdoor chairs and table
- ❖ 1 grassed area

HINT! You might want to use symbols and a key rather than writing in all the plant names by hand.

Eg: Large tree ◇   Shrub △   Seedling □

Design your own place to study

Design your own TAFE or university campus. Use the headings below to make a detailed map which shows buildings, classrooms and other facilities. Remember to use clear handwriting, drawing and labelling to make your map easy to understand. You can do this activity on paper or as a 3-dimensional model.

Your map should include the following:

- the name of your TAFE or university campus
- 3 main buildings
- 5 portable classrooms
- 2 practical workshops
- 3 staircases and / or lifts
- gardens and grassed areas
- sporting facilities
- a computer lab
- a library
- an office or reception area
- a cafeteria
- a book shop
- a student lounge
- parking areas for cars and bikes
- the closest main road
- the closest bus, tram or train station

Payments and allowances

Find out about each of the payments and allowances below. Research who is eligible, how much you receive, how you apply and any other important details.

- Austudy / Abstudy

- Youth Allowance

- Disability Support Pension

- Health Care Card

- Pensioner Concession card

- Newstart Allowance

- Remote Area Allowance

- Telephone Allowance

- Fares Allowance

- Rent Assistance

- Mobility Allowance

- Special Employment Advance

- Transition to Independent Living Allowance

What can I learn next?

Choose four of the careers from the list below, and find out about the sort of study you would need to do to work in that area. You may need to use resources such as the internet, a job support agency, your careers teacher, TAFE or university course guides or the library.

Find out about:

- Pre-requisites (do you need to have a pass in certain subjects or year levels?)
- Where the course is offered
- If you can do a traineeship or apprenticeship
- What the qualification is called
- How long you need to study
- Other related career areas

Maybe a traineeship?

Sail maker	Vet	Hairdresser
Police officer	Pool lifeguard	Pilot
Gardener	Roof tiler	Brick layer
DJ	Teacher	Truck driver
Fashion designer	Writer	Nurse
Web-page designer	Electrician	Painter
Chef	Retail sales assistant	Personal trainer
Welder	Print maker	Computer technician

Places to learn as an adult

Sometimes people are able to study close to home, but sometimes they need to travel to do the course they are interested in. Use your research skills to find out about some local, regional and interstate study options. The headings below should help you with your research.

A local TAFE	**A local university**
Name:	Name:
Street address:	Street address:
Phone number:	Phone number:
Website:	Website:
One courses offered there:	One courses offered there:
A TAFE more than 100 km from home	**A university more than 100 km from home**
Name:	Name:
Street address:	Street address:
Phone number:	Phone number:
Website:	Website:
One courses offered there:	One courses offered there:
A TAFE in another state	**A university in another state**
Name:	Name:
Street address:	Street address:
Phone number:	Phone number:
Website:	Website:
One courses offered there:	One courses offered there:

Types of training

There are lots of different types of study and training you can do once you leave school. Research each of the types of study or training listed in the box below.

You need to find out:

- What job areas are usually covered
- Advantages
- Disadvantages
- Likely costs
- If you receive any on the job training

For each of these training or study types:

- Traineeship

- Apprenticeship

- Short course at a neighbourhood house

- Short course at a TAFE

- Part or full time study at a TAFE

- Part or full time study at a university

- Part or full time study at a private college or

  institute

Unit 3 Out of Work: Learning checklist   **Name:**

This checklist allows you to keep track of the worksheets and activities that you have agreed to complete with the help and support of your teacher. Once you have agreed on the activities you are going to do for this unit, you can use the checklist as a tool for remembering what you need to do and for keeping a record of your achievements.

Worksheet / activity	Tick if chosen	Completion date	Checked
3.2 What does it mean?			
3.3 What do they do?			
3.4 What is missing?			
3.5 Words with two meanings			
3.6 Same sound, different spelling			
3.7 Words for work			
3.8 Job matching			
3.9 The right words for the right job			
3.10 True or false?			
3.11 How well did you read?			
3.12 How do you see it?			
3.13 Job interest areas			
3.14 Job categories			
3.15 About me			
3.16 Resumes			
3.17 Job application letter 1			
3.18 Job application letter 2			
3.19 Writing using key words			
3.20 Dangers at work			
3.21 About that job			
3.22 How would you apply?			
3.23 Job interests quiz			
3.24 What skills do you need?			
3.25 How to fail a job interview			
3.26 Common job interview questions			
3.27 What to do when you're not working			
3.28 Make a map			
3.29 Design a garden			
3.30 Design your own place to study			
3.31 Payments and allowances			
3.32 What can I learn next?			
3.33 Places to learn as an adult			
3.34 Types of training			

Unit 4: Moving Out

Before reading the story

Pre-reading activities are useful for all students before beginning a new unit of work. Activities such as these will help teachers establish the level of student understanding of basic concepts contained within the story, and give students a framework for topics to be covered during the unit.

1. Check that students are familiar with the main concepts and ideas they will encounter in the story. Examples might include:
    *   Renting or buying a house
    *   The concept of moving out of home
    *   Important relationships such as parents, girlfriend/boyfriend, partner
    *   Growing up
    *   Expectations of parents and how these may differ from those of their children

2. Discuss key words and phrases from the story and check that students are familiar with their meanings. Examples might include:
    *   real-estate agent
    *   professionally cleaned
    *   packing
    *   moving in together
    *   parents
    *   married
    *   grown up
    *   responsibility
    *   lonely

3. Talk about embarrassing things that parents/carers/siblings have done that students can remember. Be careful to manage this conversation in a way that ensures students who do not have parents at home do not feel singled out or unable to participate in the activity.

4. Talk about life stages from the point of view of students. Where do they see themselves in two, three, five or ten years time? Will they be living in the same place? Will their important relationships have changed?

5. Ask for students' views on living with someone before marriage. Discuss how this varies from one culture to another and from one period of time to another. Be aware of the power of unspoken messages with this activity, and try to avoid giving views that appear to judge or value one living situation over another. This activity may not be suitable for some groups, depending on age, background or religious beliefs.

About the story

Growing up and moving out. Most teenagers are desperate to do both as quickly as possible. To break away from the restrictions of parents and rules and always having to be home on time. To be able to decide for yourself what you want to cook for dinner. To be able to choose the channel on the TV without having to watch the news first. To be able to leave your clothes on the floor for a week and not pick them up. And surely most parents are just as happy to see the back of their teenagers as well? Or are they?

In **Moving Out** you will meet Gina and Jake. They are about to move out together into a small rented house. But first Jake has to manage to squeeze all his belongings into some already overflowing boxes. And Gina has to somehow convince her mother that she is grown up enough to manage on her own.

- Does Jake manage to get all his belongings to the new house?

- Does Gina persuade her mother that everything will be all right?

- Does Jake's Dad tell him how he really feels about him growing up?

- Does moving day go without a hitch?

- How do Jake and Gina eventually talk Gina's mum into going home?

Read **Moving Out** and find out.

Moving Out

Jake sits on the floor of his room surrounded by boxes and piles of clothes. He picks up a jumper, folds it carefully and adds it to the growing pile of 'things to take' on the bed. Then he picks it up again, unfolds it and places it firmly in the 'things to leave behind' pile next to the door. He sighs and looks around his room. Every drawer is open and the floor is covered with books, clothes, posters and the assorted clutter of a lifetime. How do people ever manage to sort out what they need to take when they are moving out of home for the first time and what they can leave behind for Mum to get rid of? How is he supposed to know what is important and what is not? Is Gina going through all this at her place? Should he take food with him? Will Gina cook or will she expect him to do it? He sighs again and scoops up an armload of assorted socks, jocks, T-shirts and trackies and tips them all into a box. Then he balances his skateboard, one sneaker, and a packet of computer disks on top. He lifts the box and groans in disgust as the bottom falls out and the contents spill onto the floor.

* * * * * * * *

At the same time as Jake is battling with his belongings, Gina is sitting at her kitchen table listening to the latest in a long series of instructions from her mother. Her long, dark hair is pulled back in a red scrunchie, and she tugs idly at a few loose strands hanging down by her cheek as her mother talks. Mrs V has been against the idea of Jake and Gina moving in together from the first moment it was suggested. To her way of thinking, boys and girls belong at home with their parents until they get married. End of story. But now that her baby girl has decided to move out, Mrs V is determined to make the best of it. She adds a recipe for making gravy to the bulging folder on the table and says to Gina, 'Now remember, heat the mixture gently; gravy can't be rushed like you do most things Gina.'

Gina grits her teeth and replies, 'Yes, Mum I remember. I can cook, you know. And stop worrying, Jake and I will be fine, honestly.'

Mrs V gurgles into her coffee mug, then splutters, 'Cook! Gina, I have seen you leave the milk out of mashed potatoes. I have seen you burn cheese on toast. I have seen you boil soup so hard it curdles. I have even, on one never to be forgotten occasion, seen you try to add the egg to a chocolate cake *after it was already cooked!* And you tell me not to worry – you can cook!'

'But Mum, that was when I was a kid. I'm an adult now. Jake and I know what we're doing. You just have to accept that we've grown up.'

'Hmmm,' mutters Mrs V. 'I just hope you know what being a grown up really means, Gina.'

Mrs V looks towards the door, as if checking that a spy has not suddenly slipped in when she wasn't watching. Gina half expects her to lift the tablecloth and look underneath as well. She knows what is coming next. In fact, she is surprised it has taken her mother this long to raise the topic.

'Now Gina lovey, I know you are *almost* a grown woman, but there was one other thing I wanted to talk to you about.'

Gina raises her eyes to the roof. 'Oh Mum. We don't have to talk about that, do we?' But there is no stopping her mother once she is on this track.

'Gina lovey, I just wanted to make sure that you and Jake were … you know …' She pauses for a moment and Gina watches her face redden. She whispers to Gina, '*Careful.*'

Gina can't help herself. 'Careful of what, Mum?'

'Babies, Gina,' replies Mrs V.

Gina smiles. The way her mum talks about babies, it is as if they are small alien creatures that can sneak into the house through the cracks in the floorboards. Mind you, thinks Gina, most of the babies she had seen did look pretty much like aliens. All scrunched up and scrawny, with funny red faces and pokey-out ears. Gina decides to head this conversation off before it goes too far.

'It's okay Mum, you don't have to worry about being a grandma just yet. I'm on the pill.'

'Ayaya,' says Mrs V, and starts rapidly flicking through the pages of the recipe books on the table. She waggles her finger at Gina. 'Just you be careful, my girl. You can't always rely on boys to do the right thing you know.'

* * * * * * *

Jake has finally managed to squash most of the boxes into his dad's trailer. The boot of the car is full, and what hasn't fitted into the boot is piled up on the back seat. His surfboard is strapped to the roof. His mum is standing in the driveway, her arms folded across her chest. His dad cuts the power to the lawn mower he has been pushing through the long grass on the nature strip and comes over to join them. Ginger, the cat that Jake was given for his tenth birthday, winds her long tail around his legs, purring softly to herself. Jake looks at the three of them. He can't believe he is finally about to start his life as an adult. His mum smiles at him, and he is sure he can see a tear starting to form in the corner of her eye. He puts his arm around her and wonders how to put all this into words. How to say thank you to the two people who have supported him through tough times at school, encouraged his artwork, helped him find a job, made Gina feel like she is one of the family, been there whenever he needed a hand. He turns to them both.

'Mum, Dad …,' he begins.

Suddenly his Dad yells. 'The cricket! Look at the time! The first test started this arvo, and I'm missing it!' He thrusts his hand towards Jake. 'See you, son. Your mum and I will be round tomorrow to see how you're settling in. Gotta go.'

With that, his Dad races up the driveway to the house, Ginger following happily behind him.

* * * * * * *

Gina and her mother arrive at the house first and park in the driveway. They follow the path that leads across the grass towards the house, then veers suddenly left before stopping at a low brick wall.

'I know,' says Gina stepping neatly through a flower bed. 'In boring houses the path leads to the front door. But why be the same as everyone else in the street?'

'Ayaya,' mutters Mrs V.

Gina pulls a face as her mother slides her hands into a pair of bright yellow laundry gloves and fixes her hair back in a scarf. She slides the sleeves of her 'housework dress' up to her elbows and frowns at the house in general. 'Show me the laundry and bathroom, Gina. It will need a good clean before you can use it.'

'It's clean, Mum. The estate agent said the house had been professionally cleaned after the last people left.'

Mrs V looks around her.

'Professionally cleaned, bah! Who ever heard of a professional who could clean anything!'

She marches through the house looking for the bathroom. Gina watches her, wondering how long it will take before her mum works out the layout of the odd little house. Finally Mrs V flings back a curtain at the end of the hallway, and cries, 'Ahah! The bathroom, here she is.'

Her gazes falls upon a rag that has been left hanging over the edge of the bath. She seizes it triumphantly.

'See. They don't even pick up after themselves, these professionals.'

By the time Gina hears Jake's car pull up outside, Mrs V has scrubbed the floors, polished the already spotless sink and shower, and disinfected the kitchen.

Gina jumps up and rushes out to greet Jake, who is struggling to balance a large cardboard box in one arm and a pair of footy boots in the other. She flings her arms around his shoulders and knocks him to the ground.

'Oh Jake,' says Gina apologetically. 'You shouldn't try to carry so much at once.'

'Thhrts rkay,' mumbles Jake from under the surfboard. 'I needed to put it all down anyway.'

Gina and Jake walk in to the house together. Jake has his arm around Gina's shoulder, and Gina has taken responsibility for the box. She places it carefully on the floor in the main bedroom next to her own pile of belongings then walks back to the car. For the next hour, they make a series of trips from the cars to the house. Mrs V watches in amazement as every room in the tiny house is filled. Boxes sit on chairs, under tables and along the hall. Packets of noodles mix with tea bags in the kitchen and the laundry sink is soon filled with dirty work socks, old T-shirts and overalls. Gina walks into the laundry and giggles. 'Hey Jake, I don't suppose you thought about doing your washing before you put it all in your bag, did you?'

'Yeah, yeah, I ran out of time, that's all,' says Jake. He grins as water gushes across the floor from where Gina is trying without success to fit the washing machine hose to the tap. He takes the hose from her and clicks it into place.

'Since when did you become perfect, anyway?' he asks.

Finally the cars and trailer have been emptied and some order restored to the house. Gina puts a 'Welcome' mat at the front door, then steps over it and wipes her feet on the carpet. She goes to sit next to Jake, who is struggling to make conversation with her mother.

'So, who do you think will win the election next week?' asks Jake.

'I don't follow politics much,' says Mrs V.

'How about the cricket? Do you think Australia is going to win the test?' asks Jake.

'I don't watch the cricket,' says Mrs V.

'Did you see the pub on the highway before you turned into our street? They've got heaps of pokies there and they have a two-for-one meal deal every Friday. We found a voucher for it in the paper,' says Jake.

'My cousin in Brisbane lost all his payout money on the pokies,' answers Mrs V.

'Oh,' says Jake.

There is silence for a while.

'So, it's quite a long drive back to your place, isn't it Mrs V?' says Jake eventually. The hint seems lost on Mrs V, who wipes her face with her apron then lifts her large frame from the chair and walks across the kitchen. She fills the kettle before answering.

'It is a long drive,' she says to Jake. 'Better have a cuppa before I drive back I guess.'

Gina and Jake look at each other in despair. Mrs V sits back comfortably in her chair and smiles at them.

An hour and a half and three cups of tea later, Mrs V pushes her chair back from the table. Gina and Jake look at each other hopefully.

Mrs V gathers up her bag, gloves and scarf and looks around the house.

'Now pet,' she says to Gina. 'I'll just pop into your room and make your bed for you before I go.'

'No!' says Gina. 'Enough Mum! I think Jake and I can manage to make a bed ourselves. Besides ...' she giggles, then stops as Jake pokes her in the ribs.

He walks over to where her mum is standing by the bedroom door, her bag clutched to her chest. He recognises the same sad look that he had seen on his own mother's face only a few hours earlier. He knows that Mrs V is not trying to be difficult, she is just feeling lonely at the thought of losing her youngest daughter. He suspects also that she is dreading going home to a house that would be empty for the first time since the death of Gina's father earlier in the year.

He puts his arms around her and hugs her tightly. Gina looks at them both in surprise.

'It'll be OK, Mrs V,' he whispers quietly. He feels her trying hard not to cry, then she draws her breath in and pulls away from him and pats him arm.

'Ahh', she says. 'You're a good boy, Jake. Your mother must be very proud of you, I think. Very proud.'

She fishes in her bag for a tissue and blows her nose loudly.

'How about you come around for dinner tomorrow night, Mrs V?' he asks. 'You can come and show us how to cook a roast dinner. We could even open a bottle of bubbly to celebrate moving into our new house.'

'Of course,' replies Mrs V with a smile. 'I would love to come for dinner. So long as you don't let Gina make the gravy though.'

She winks at Jake as Gina opens her mouth to protest.

'Always in a rush, that girl, always in a rush!'

She pats Jake's arm again then steps happily over the doormat and across the grass to her car. Jake follows her and gets into his own car. He waves at Gina then puts the car into reverse. The wheels are still angled sharply towards the house, and one wheel of the trailer is in the gutter at the edge of the driveway. Gina puts her hand up to point to the trailer wheels, and Jake waves at her again.

Gina watches helplessly as Jake reverses the car and trailer across a garden bed, destroying several small plants. Red-faced, he drives forward, then reverses and tries again. He finally stops the car with the trailer resting up against the front fence. There is silence for a moment, followed by a splintering sound and a crash as part of the fence gives way. Mrs V sits watching him in the rear view mirror, impatiently revving her engine. She turns her engine off again, and climbs out of the car.

'Ayaya,' she mutters to herself. 'Whoever heard of a boy who couldn't reverse a trailer?'

She pushes Jake out of the way, and carefully straightens the trailer then backs it expertly down the drive.

Gina and Jake stand on the verandah listening to the screech of tyres as Mrs V rounds the corner onto the highway and drives away. They are alone in their new house at last.

Activities for beginning readers

These activities will be useful for students who have limited reading skills, and who will prefer to listen to the story rather than reading it independently. The activities cover a range of presentation types in order to cater for a variety of preferred student learning styles. The use of concrete objects can help students to retain information presented during these activities, and can be used as a way of teaching key words from the story.

1. **Make a poster of real estate advertisements** – divide the poster into two halves. One half shows advertisements of properties to rent, and the other shows properties for sale.

2. **House plan** – Use a piece of butchers' paper and roughly sketch out the floor plan of a house. Ask students to draw in pictures of furniture and other important items that they would need to have in a house.

3. **Supermarket visit** – Visit a supermarket and compare the prices of a typical trolley of groceries. This activity can also be done using catalogues or an online shopping website.

4. **Where do you stand?** – For this game, ask students to stand along an imaginary line according to how strongly they agree or disagree with a particular statement. Statements to try might include:

    *   People should be married before they move in together
    *   Your parents should have a say in who you choose to marry
    *   Men should do all the physical jobs around the house
    *   Women should do all the cooking and cleaning
    *   People should be able to make you do something if they think it is for your own good
    *   Your parents should help you choose your first house

    Obviously this activity should be varied according to the particular needs, values and backgrounds of your group. For some groups, statements such as these will be thought provoking and interesting, whilst for others they could be highly distressing.

5. **Jobs for the boys / jobs for the girls?** – Make cards with a variety of household tasks written on them, with a picture of each task drawn underneath. Ask students to sort the cards into piles according to who they think should be responsible for each one. A variation on this activity is to ask students to sort the cards according to who does each job in their current living situation.

6. **Budgets** – Ask students to help make a list of costs associated with running a household. These can be written or drawn onto a whiteboard or sheet of paper. Estimate the costs of the various items, and talk about what each item means. Some students may not be familiar with words such as insurance, rent, electricity, gas, car servicing etc so make sure you discuss these.

7. **Leave it in or throw it out?** – Bring in a pile of objects and ask students to help you sort them into two piles. One pile is for items that they think you should throw out, and the other is for items you should keep. Examples might include:

- an old jumper
- a good pair of socks
- a primary school book
- a sticker
- a scratched CD
- a current diary
- a diary from a few years ago
- a ripped photo
- a pen that doesn't work
- an empty bottle of dishwashing liquid

This activity can be useful for helping students to become familiar with the names of common household items, and also to increase their understanding of words such as 'broken', 'old', 'out of date', 'new' and 'damaged'.

8. **My ideal house** – Ask students to draw a picture of, or write a paragraph about their ideal house. Encourage creativity rather than reality with this activity, as you are likely to be rewarded with houses that would make a movie star jealous!

9. **Reality check** – Some students have an eye for impressive entertainment systems, without necessarily understanding the true costs involved. Take your group on a visit to the electrical department of a department store and check the prices of a few items. You may find there are some horrified expressions at the end of this activity!

Word categories 1

Organise each of the words from the word list into their correct categories. Then create a sentence using one word from each category. Try to make your sentence as interesting as possible.

sits	red
Gina	makes
cleans	jumps
house	book
listens	bath
box	smiles
socks	quietly
Jake	cooks
boots	hears
neatly	loudly
funny	long
tough	

Actions

Descriptions

People, places or objects

_____

_____

_____

_____

Word categories 2

Organise each of the words from the word list into their correct categories. Then write a paragraph using at least two words from each category. Your paragraph should be 3 or more sentences in length.

glances	pile
rapidly	carefully
folds	grits
gravy	woman
gloves	spotless
happily	expertly
takes	spills
floor	overalls
lifts	smiles
stands	Mrs V
mum	squashes
knocks	odd
comfortably	

Actions

Descriptions

People, places or objects

_____
_____
_____
_____
_____
_____
_____
_____
_____

What does it mean?

Use your dictionary or write your own definitions for each of these words.

- professional

- assorted

- landscaping

- disinfect

- support

- election

- pokies

- reverses

- verandah

- dread

- concrete

- agent

- gushes

- voucher

Word opposites

See if you can think of words which are opposite in meaning to the words in the list. You may find that adding a prefix such as **un** or **dis** to some of the words will reverse the meaning of the original word.

1. professional   _____

2. organised   _____

3. successful   _____

4. found   _____

5. before   _____

6. welcome   _____

7. dirty   _____

8. quietly   _____

9. happily   _____

10. empty   _____

11. covered   _____

12. first   _____

13. encouraged   _____

Add an ending

Complete this table by adding the correct ending to each of these base words. Be careful – the spelling of some of the words needs to be changed before you add the ending. Can you work out which ones?

Base word	Add *s* or *es*	Add *d* or *ed*	Add *ing*
lift			
heat			
glance			
talk			
smile			
worry			
flick			
fit			
settle			
follow			
pull			
show			
look			
clean			
watch			

Which word is correct?

When we change the spelling of a word to mean something which has happened in the past, we say we are using the **past tense** of the word. Sometimes we add a **d** or an **ed** to create a past tense word, but sometimes we have to change the whole word.

Circle the correct past tenses for each of the words in the list below.

1. **stand**   standed   stood

2. **take**   took   taked

3. **make**   maked   made

4. **say**   said   sayed

5. **slide**   slidded   slid

6. **hear**   heared   heard

7. **fall**   fell   falled

8. **fling**   flinged   flung

9. **think**   thought   thinked

10. **see**   seed   saw

11. **drive**   drived   drove

12. **know**   knew   knowed

13. **come**   comed   came

14. **feel**   felt   feeled

15. **bring**   bringed   brought

> **Hint:** Try saying each word in a sentence to check if it is correct.

Word race

How quickly can you find a word from the story for each of these categories?

1. Type of clothing _____

2. Person's name _____

3. Type of food _____

4. Something you sit at _____

5. Part of a house _____

6. A very small person _____

7. Something you read _____

8. It goes on your foot _____

9. Use this for surfing _____

10. Covers your hair _____

11. Covers a window _____

12. Use this to cut grass _____

13. A colour _____

14. Ginger is one of these _____

15. Used to wash clothes _____

16. A sport _____

17. A type of gambling _____

18. Going backwards _____

19. A noise from tyres _____

20. A type of road _____

Your time : _____ mins _____ secs

True or false?

Read through the story and decide which of these statements are true and which are false.

1.	Jake puts his bike on the roof of his car.	**TRUE**	**FALSE**
2.	Jake owns a skateboard.	**TRUE**	**FALSE**
3.	Gina's mum gives her a quiche recipe.	**TRUE**	**FALSE**
4.	Jake's dad drives him to the house.	**TRUE**	**FALSE**
5.	Gina thinks that babies look like aliens.	**TRUE**	**FALSE**
6.	Jake's dad goes inside to watch the footy.	**TRUE**	**FALSE**
7.	Mrs V wears blue gloves.	**TRUE**	**FALSE**
8.	Jake gets to the house before Gina.	**TRUE**	**FALSE**
9.	Gina's mum and Mrs V are the same person.	**TRUE**	**FALSE**
10.	Gina has trouble with the washing machine.	**TRUE**	**FALSE**
11.	Jake has trouble backing the trailer.	**TRUE**	**FALSE**
12.	Mrs V knows someone who lost his money playing pokies.	**TRUE**	**FALSE**
13.	Mrs V offers to make Gina and Jake's bed.	**TRUE**	**FALSE**
14.	Jake invites Gina's mum for dinner.	**TRUE**	**FALSE**
15.	Gina is on the pill.	**TRUE**	**FALSE**
16.	Jake has a cat called Felix.	**TRUE**	**FALSE**
17.	Gina knocks Jake over when she rushes outside to meet him.	**TRUE**	**FALSE**

How well did you read?

These questions will test how well you read the story **Moving Out**. You may need to look back at the story for some of your answers.

1. What happens to the box that Jake is packing in his room?

   _____

2. What does Gina's mum want to talk to Gina about?

   _____

3. What does Jake have strapped to the roof of his car?

   _____

4. What recipe does Gina's mum give to Gina?

   _____

5. What does Jake's dad want to watch on TV?

   _____

6. What has Gina's mum cleaned before Jake arrives at the house?

   _____

7. What is the name of Jake's cat?

   _____

8. What day of the week is the two-for-one deal at the pub?

   _____

9. How many cups of tea does Mrs V drink before she leaves?

   _____

10. What colour are the gloves that Mrs V brings with her to the house?

    _____

11. What is written on the mat that Gina puts at the front door?

    _____

Why do you think?

For these questions, you need to think about why things happened the way they did in the story. You may find it is useful to talk to a partner about some of the questions.

1. Why do you think Jake's dad rushes inside to watch the cricket just before Jake leaves?

    _____

    _____

2. Why do you think Gina's mum wants to talk to her about babies?

    _____

    _____

3. Why do you think Gina's mum takes so long to leave the house once they have unpacked?

    _____

    _____

4. Why do you think Jake is worried about whether he should take food with him to the house?

    _____

    _____

5. Why do you think Jake invites Gina's mum to stay for dinner?

    _____

    _____

6. Why do you think Gina does not want her mum to make her bed for her?

    _____

    _____

7. Why do you think Jake has trouble making conversation with Gina's mum?

    _____

    _____

Writing an instruction list

For each of these household jobs, write a set of step-by-step instructions that are easy to read, understand and follow. You may need to research some of the jobs at home. Use brief dot points for your instructions.

Example: <u>Checking which day the bins are emptied at your new house</u>

Step 1 – Check that you know your new address.

Step 2 – Have a pen and some paper ready.

Step 3 – Find the phone number for the local council.

Step 4 – Call the council and say that you have just moved into the area and you need to know which day the bins are emptied.

Step 5 – Write down the day and any other information you are given, such as whether the collection is weekly or fortnightly.

Step 6 – Put the information in a safe place.

- Changing a light globe

- Checking the battery in a smoke alarm

- Setting the time on a clock radio

- Turning on the hot water service

- Connecting the washing machine

- Recording a new message on an answering machine

- Setting up a computer

- Organising the kitchen cupboards

- Changing your address with the gas company

Take or leave behind?

You are moving out of home for the first time. You have left your packing to the last minute and you can hear the truck pull up outside. You only have a few minutes to pack your ten most precious possessions and five very practical things into a box.

What will you take with you?

Precious and practical
things box
DO NOT THROW
OUT

Precious things

1. _____
2. _____
3. _____
4. _____
5. _____
6. _____
7. _____
8. _____
9. _____
10. _____

Practical things

1. _____
2. _____
3. _____
4. _____
5. _____

Personal details

Imagine you are moving out of home. You want to make sure everyone can find you at your new house. Think about who you would need to tell, and how you would write out your new address and phone number.

List five friends you would need to give your details to:

1. _____

2. _____

3. _____

4. _____

5. _____

List three companies you would need to give your new details to:

1. _____

2. _____

3. _____

Write your current personal details here:

Name _____

Address _____

Postcode _____

Phone number _____

Make up a set of personal details for your imaginary new house:

Name _____

Address _____

Postcode _____

Phone number _____

Being careful with chemicals

For each of these household items, describe any dangers such as contact with skin or eyes. Where should you keep each of them in the house?

HOUSEHOLD ITEM	DANGER	STORAGE
laundry detergent		
dishwashing liquid		
bathroom soap		
fly spray		
floor cleaner		
mouthwash		
toothpaste		
nail-polish remover		
craft glue		
hair spray		
methylated spirits		
mineral turpentine		
shampoo		
conditioner		
shoe polish		
car polish		
shaving cream		
paint		
vinegar		

Household safety quiz

DANGER!

How safe is your house? Do this quick quiz for your own house, or for a house that you can imagine yourself living in sometime in the future.

1. How many windows are there in your house?

2. How many windows can be locked?

3. How many doors are there in your house?

4. How many doors can be locked?

5. How many smoke alarms are there in your house?

6. When did you last check the smoke alarm batteries?

7. Do you have an evacuation plan and meeting place for your house?

8. Do you have a fire blanket or fire extinguisher in your kitchen?

9. Do you know how to call the police, fire brigade or ambulance?

10. What other things can you think of that would make your house safer?

Using appliances

Imagine you have just moved into a fully furnished apartment. Your landlady has left a note explaining three things to remember for each appliance. What do you think she has written?

Dishwasher

Stereo system

Video player

Washing machine

Microwave oven

Convection oven

Clothes dryer

Vacuum cleaner

About the characters

Write a paragraph or some dot points about each of these characters, and draw a picture of how you imagine they might look. Read back through the story to remind yourself about each character.

Jake

Jake's dad

Gina

Mrs V

Jobs for the boys, jobs for the girls?

Work with a partner to construct an argument for or against the statement in the box below. Think about how you will argue your case, and how you will convince your audience that you are right.

> *"Boys should be responsible for mowing the lawn, putting the bins out, walking the dog and collecting the mail."*
>
> *"Girls should be responsible for washing the clothes and dishes, cooking the meals, doing the shopping and cleaning the house."*

You are arguing: **FOR**   **AGAINST** (circle one)

Main points: Speaker 1

1.

2.

3.

4.

Main points: Speaker 2

1.

2.

3.

4.

Conclusion:

You're too young to move out

Work with a partner to construct an argument for or against the statement in the box below. Think about how you will argue your case, and how you will convince your audience that you are right.

> *"Your parents say that you are too young to move out of home yet. You should wait another year or two, or at least until you have been working for a few years and have grown up a bit more. You are not responsible and mature enough to move out of home."*

You are arguing: **FOR**   **AGAINST** (circle one)

Main points: Speaker 1

1.

2.

3.

4.

Main points: Speaker 2

1.

2.

3.

4.

Conclusion:

'Australianisms' poem

There are lots of words that have become part of Australian slang, or that have become known as 'Australianisms'. In the story, Jake talks about opening a bottle of bubbly, and Mrs V wants a 'cuppa'.

Write a poem using as many Australianisms as you can find. There are some examples to help you get started.

Australian slang

There are lots of words and phrases that are part of Australian slang. Some are known throughout Australia, while others are only used in particular places or by certain groups of people. See how many of these words and phrases you know. Write the meaning for each on a separate sheet of paper. Can you add some more words of your own?

> The yuppie greenie lost her sunnies when we stopped to take some happy snaps, then whinged all the way home!

freebie	sunnies	yuppie
PJs	mozzie	trackies
Buckley's	stubby	ute
feral	stoked	BYO
mockies	bubbly	whinger
hand-me-downs	dole	snag
belting	cellar-dwellers	bogan
greenie	raw prawn	petrol head
brekkie	barbie	brollie
beaut	nerd	bickie
brickie	sparkie	chook
busted	happy snaps	nibblies
wag	arvo	cobber
bloke	chick	vegies

Hot topics for discussion

Discuss one of these topics with a partner or in a small group. Are your opinions the same as or different from others in the group?

Teenagers are not capable of living in a house on their own.

Girls are better at housework than boys.

People should wait until they are married before they move in together.

It's okay to take your washing home for your mum to do.

Renting is better than buying.

Girls don't need to know how to fix things around the house so long as they have a boy around to help them.

Design your own house

Design your own house using the prompts below. Remember to use neat, accurate labelling and pictures or symbols to make your house design easy to read. Use abbreviations where possible: eg **BIR , main BR.**

You will need:

A grey lead pencil
A ruler
An eraser
A fine line black pen and coloured pencils for your final design
Some scrap paper for your drafts
A sheet of A3 paper for your final design

Your design must have:

- at least three bedrooms
- at least one bathroom
- at least two toilets
- a kitchen
- a laundry
- a lounge room or study
- a family room or rumpus room
- a front door
- a back door
- a driveway
- a front and back garden or courtyard
- a pool or tennis court
- parking space for two cars

Real estate language

Real estate advertisements can be difficult to understand unless you have learnt some of the abbreviations that are used. Do some research into each of the abbreviations in the list, and then write your own advertisement for a property to rent or buy.

BIR _____ (type of wardrobe)

OSP _____ (for your car)

OFP _____ (heating)

LUG _____ (space for one car)

DLUG _____ (space for two cars)

B/R _____ (place to sleep)

GDH _____ (heating)

A/C _____ (cooling)

WB _____ (building material)

Solar htd. _____ (for your pool)

STCA _____ (ask the council)

Mod. Con. _____ (very modern)

Your own house advertisement

What does it cost to move out?

Moving out of home can be expensive. Do some research to find out about the costs in the list below. You can use any of the tools listed for your research, and you can present your information using words, pictures or both.

Research tools
White pages phone book
Yellow pages phone book
Local phone book
Street directory
Shopping catalogues
Newspapers
Real estate agent listings
Ask a friend or relative

How much does it cost to:

Buy a new fridge _____

Buy a second-hand television _____

Buy a new washing machine _____

Buy a set of cutlery (knives, forks and spoons) _____

Buy a set of crockery (plates, bowls and cups) _____

Buy a set of linen for a double bed
(doona cover, sheets, pillowcases) _____

Do a load of washing at the Laundromat _____

Rent a 2 bedroom apartment in an outer suburb _____

Rent a 3 bedroom house in an outer suburb _____

Rent a 2 bedroom apartment in the inner city area _____

Rent a 3 bedroom house in the inner city area _____

Connect a telephone line _____

Have a television aerial installed _____

Favourite recipes

For this activity, you need to put together a collection of recipes that would be useful if you moved out of home. You can look in recipe books, on the internet, or ask someone you know to write out a favourite recipe.

Find a recipe for two of these meals:

- Lamb roast with potatoes, pumpkin and carrots
- Fried rice
- Thai fish cakes
- Russian salad
- Lamb samosas

Find a recipe for two of these dishes:

- Baked potato with your choice of toppings
- Nachos with cream, cheese and salsa
- Scrambled eggs
- Mashed potatoes
- Coleslaw

Find a recipe from two of these countries:

- Thailand
- Greece
- India
- Italy
- England
- Spain

Fast food near your house

Do some research on a fast-food or take-away outlet that is close to your house. Complete the tasks in the box below for one of the types of fast food listed at the bottom of the page.

TASKS

1. **Name** – Find out the name of the restaurant / fast food outlet

2. **Address** – Find out the address of the restaurant / fast food outlet

3. **Phone** – Find out the phone number of the restaurant / fast food outlet

4. **Menu** – Collect a menu (if available)

5. **Most expensive** – Write out the name and price for the most expensive item on the menu

6. **Cheapest** – Write out the name and price for the cheapest item on the menu

7. **Sample order** – Write out a sample order for a dinner for four people

8. **Cost** – Work out the cost for the dinner using the menu

Fast-food / take-away restaurants

- Chinese, Vietnamese or Thai restaurant
- Indian restaurant
- Pizza restaurant
- Fish and chip shop
- Hamburger cafe
- Noodle bar

Unit 4 Moving Out: Learning checklist   Name:

This checklist allows you to keep track of the worksheets and activities that you have agreed to complete with the help and support of your teacher. Once you have agreed on the activities you are going to do for this unit, you can use the checklist as a tool for remembering what you need to do and for keeping a record of your achievements.

Worksheet / activity	Tick if chosen	Completion date	Checked
4.2 Word categories 1			
4.3 Word categories 2			
4.4 What does it mean?			
4.5 Word opposites			
4.6 Add an ending			
4.7 Which word is correct?			
4.8 Word race			
4.9 True or false?			
4.10 How well did you read?			
4.11 Why do you think?			
4.12 Writing an instruction list			
4.13 Take or leave behind?			
4.14 Personal details			
4.15 Being careful with chemicals			
4.16 Household safely quiz			
4.17 Using appliances			
4.18 About the characters			
4.19 Jobs for the boys			
4.20 You're too young to move out			
4.21 'Australianisms' poem			
4.22 Australian slang			
4.23 Hot topics for discussion			
4.24 Design your own house			
4.25 Real-estate language			
4.26 What does it cost to move out?			
4.27 Favourite recipes			
4.28 Fast food near your house			

Answers

Pak and Jimmy's Place

1.2 Matching words
trolley, pizza, different, always, shallow, window, sometimes, afford, girlfriend, showing, breakfast, cereal, weekend

1.3 Missing letters
1. Monday 2. Friday 3. swim 4. breakfast 5. salad 6. train 7. wallet 8. lonely 9. rush 10. scrambled 11. morning 12. favourite 13. kettle 14. bedroom 15. trolley 16. bathroom 17. chocolate

1.4 Alphabetical order
1. although, both, cheaper, deal, eat, favourite 2. bathroom, bedroom, kitchen, laundry, lounge room, toilet 3. fishing, football, movie, swim, television, video 4. bacon, cereal, egg, jam, milk, toast 5. bacon, bread, cereal, coffee, margarine, milk 6. save, share, shower, so, sometimes, street 7. that, the, then, there, they, this 8. pineapple, pizza, splash, swim, week, work

1.6 Change the meaning
1. telling 2. reading 3. walking 4. living 5. visiting 6. sharing 7. hiring 8. eating 9. showering 10. making 11. inviting 12. remembering 13. working

1.7 The great shopping challenge
Pak - $31.79 Jimmy - $45.19

1.8 True or false?
1. false 2. true 3. false 4. false 5. true 6. true 7. true 8. true 9. true 10. true 11. false 12. true 13. true

1.9 How well did you read?
1. Pak 2. Pak 3. Chelsea 4. yes 5. Jimmy 6. 7.45a m 7. Amanda 8. Friday

First Impressions

2.3 Word opposites
1. least 2. enemy 3. straight 4. remember 5. roughly 6. old 7. later 8. silly 9. low 10. odd 11. sit 12. backward 13. separate 14. hard.

2.4 Word endings
sixteen, trouble, country, opinion, horror, impression, anything, clumsy, experience, comfortable, teachers

2.5 Choose the correct word
1. went 2. pair 3. stuck 4. There 5. for 6. drawer 7. except 8. get 9. knew 10. too 11. breath 12. licence

2.6 Past tense
1. was 2. went 3. had 4. wore 5. chose 6. knew 7. thought 8. found 9. spent 10. asked 11. tried

2.8 Alphabetical order
1. actually, came, decided, eyes, funny, Henri 2. call, explain, listen, speak, tell whisper. 3. bothered, bus, forgotten, friends, thought, time. 4. cheeks, eyelashes, eyes, head, nose, teeth. 5. serious, she, shower, sister, smell, strange. 6. last, learn, least, like, Linh, look, lot, lurk. 7. reach, read, relevant, right, road, roundabout, rule, run.

2.9 What's that short for?
1. You have 2. did not 3. cannot 4. that is 5. do not 6. could not 7. we have 8. does not 9. I am 10. There's 11. we'll 12. hadn't 13. she's 14. hasn't 15. he's 16. haven't 17. wasn't.

2.10 True or false?
1. true 2. false 3. true 4. true 5. true 6. false 7. false 8. true 9. false 10. false

2.11 Who did what?
1. Linh 2. Brett 3. Henri 4. Brett 5. Ivan 6. Frances's sister 7. Tamiko 8. Brett

2.12 How well did you read?
1. The barbecue was organised as a fundraising activity. 2. Frances poured tomato sauce all over Brett's hand. 3. The last class of the day was Driver Education. 4. Frances had chewing gum on her skirt from the bus seat. 5. When Frances fell over in front of Brett, the two girls with him started to laugh. 6. Tamiko often gets in trouble because she says the wrong thing. 7. Frances powdered her cheeks with pink blusher. 8. Francie woke up at 6.30 am so she could get ready to go to TAFE. 9. At Henri's old school in the country, other students poured glue into his pencil case. 10. Brett has blue eyes. 11. Frances had Milo with her breakfast. 12. The class sells sausages at the barbecue. 13. At the end of the first half of the basketball game, some of the students have a cigarette.

Out of Work

3.4 What is missing?
advertisement, bus, waitress, newspaper, phone, phone number, diary, interview, motivation, address, train, wages, late, appointment, manager, negative, trainee, career

3.6 Same sound, different spelling
weight, won, dye, threw, knead, wear, reel, no, son, here, sea, wood, bee, hoarse, bean, pear, shore, sew, hole.

3.7 Words for work
Horticulture/gardening: grass, mow, weed, plant, seedling, trim, mulch, sprinkler
Hospitality/cooking: chef, chop, knife, plate, serve, prepare, lettuce, bread, boil, bake, roast, vegetables, eat, salad.
Automotive/cars: bumper, brake, panel, tyre, ignition, polish, steering, oil, road, drive, detail, windscreen.
Recreation/sports: sweat, bounce, umpire, coach, fitness, gym, aerobics, swim, tennis, football, run, cricket, weights, stretch.

3.8 Job matching
bar attendant – serves drinks in a bar; aerobics instructor – teaches fitness classes in a gym; camp worker – organises outdoor camping activities; potter – makes, decorates and fires pottery; kitchen hand – washes dishes and glassware; computer assembler – puts computer hardware together; computer operator – uses software programs on a computer; stablehand – works with horses in a racing stable; interpreter – translates one language into another; childcare worker – supervises babies and young children; telemarketer – sells products or services over the phone; nail technician – cleans, repairs and decorates fingernails; motor mechanic – repairs cars; aged care worker – cares for elderly people; panel beater – repairs car bodies and panels; real-estate agent – buys and sells property for others; interior designer – arranges indoor colour, spaces and lighting; florist – creates floral arrangements.

3.10 True or false?
1. true 2. false 3. true 4. false 5. false 6. true 7. false 8. true 9. false 10. false 11. true 12. true 13. false 14. true 15. true 16. false 17. true 18. false

3.11 How well did you read?
1. Career counsellor 2. four months 3. sometimes 4. student opinion 5. student opinion 6. outdoors, late starts, close to transport, no qualifications 7. because she had trouble ringing up about the previous job 8. afternoon shift, Rundle Street, busy cafe, training, above award wages 9. student opinion 10. 277 Fullarton Road Nth, Norwood 11. 2 pm 12. meets the group in the park 13. study or growing plants, flowers and vegetables 14. student opinion 15. they didn't want her because she was Greek 16. 7 17. Greek 18. dark pants, boots, blue shirt

Moving Out

4.2 Word categories 1
Actions – sits, makes, cleans, jumps, listens, smiles, cooks, hears **Descriptions** – red, quietly, neatly, loudly, funny, long, tough **People, places, objects** – Gina, house, book, bath, box, socks, Jake, boots.

4.3 Word categories 2
Actions – glances, folds, grits, takes, spills, lifts, smiles, stands, squashes, knocks **Descriptions** – carefully, comfortably, happily, expertly, odd **People, places, objects** – gravy, woman, gloves, floor, overalls, MrsV, mum

4.5 Word opposites
1. unprofessional 2. disorganised 3. unsuccessful 4. lost 5. after 6. unwelcome 7. clean 8. noisily 9. sadly 10. full 11. uncovered 12. last 13. discouraged

4.6 Add an ending
lifts, lifted, lifting; heats, heated, heating; glances, glanced, glancing; talks, talked, talking; smiles, smiled, smiling; worries, worried, worrying; flicks, flicked, flicking; fits, fitted, fitting; settles, settled, settling; follows, followed, following; pulls, pulled, pulling; shows, showed, showing; looks, looked, looking; cleans, cleaned, cleaning; watches, watched, watching

4.7 Which word is correct?
1. stood 2. took 3. made 4. said 5. slid 6. heard 7. fell 8. flung 9. thought 10. saw 11. drove 12. knew 13. came 14. felt 15. brought

4.9 True or false?
1. false 2. true 3. false 4. false 5. true 6. false 7. false 8. false 9. true 10. true 11. true 12. true 13. true 14. true 15. true 16. false 17. true

4.10 How well did you read?
1. bottom falls out of the box 2. safe sex 3. surfboard 4. gravy recipe 5. the cricket test match 6. floors, sink, shower, kitchen 7. Ginger 8. Fridays 9. three cups 10. yellow 11. Welcome